The Effects of Sea Mining on Amphibious Warfare

James F. Ball

NIMBLE BOOKS LLC: THE AI LAB FOR BOOK-LOVERS
~ FRED ZIMMERMAN, EDITOR ~
Humans and AI making books richer, more diverse, and more surprising.

Publishing Information

(c) 2023 Nimble Books LLC
ISBN: 978-1-60888-273-1

AI-generated Keyword Phrases

sea mining; amphibious warfare; case studies; Gallipoli; Normandy; Wonsan; Persian Gulf; Operation Desert Storm; forces involved; mining conducted; impact of mining; mine countermeasures; achievement of surprise in assault; force levels crucial for success of amphibious assaults; adequate force levels leading to successful operations; rapid and complete mine countermeasures for achieving surprise in amphibious assaults; historical context of amphibious warfare; strategic considerations of amphibious warfare; operational considerations of amphib

Publisher's Notes

This annotated edition illustrates the capabilities of the AI Lab for Book-Lovers to add context and ease-of-use to manuscripts. It includes five types of abstracts, building from simplest to more complex: TLDR (one word), ELI5, TLDR (vanilla), Scientific Style, and Action Items; three essays to increase viewpoint diversity: Grounds for Dissent, Red Team Critique, and MAGA Perspective; and Notable Passages and Nutshell Summaries for each page.

ANNOTATIONS

Publishing Information ii
AI-generated Keyword Phrases ii
Publisher's Notes ii
Abstracts iv
    TL;DR (one word) iv
    Explain It To Me Like I'm Five Years Old iv
    TL;DR (vanilla) iv
    Scientific Style iv
    Action Items v
Viewpoints vi
    Grounds for Dissent vi
    Red Team Critique vii
    MAGA Perspective viii
Page-by-Page Summaries x
Notable Passages xxi

Abstracts

TL;DR (One Word)

Amphibious.

Explain It To Me Like I'm Five Years Old

This document is a big report that looks at how mining the sea can affect wars that happen both on land and in water. It talks about some battles that happened a long time ago in places like Gallipoli, Normandy, Wonsan, and the Persian Gulf. The report looks at the different groups of people who fought in these battles, how they used mining, and how it affected their plans. It says that having enough people in your group is really important to win these battles, and

TL;DR (Vanilla)

This thesis examines the effects of sea mining on amphibious warfare through case studies. It concludes that adequate force levels and effective mine countermeasures are crucial for successful amphibious assaults. The document provides historical context, discusses strategic and operational considerations, and emphasizes the significance of mine warfare in amphibious operations.

Scientific Style

This thesis investigates the effects of sea mining on amphibious warfare through case studies of amphibious assaults at Gallipoli, Normandy, Wonsan, and the Persian Gulf during Operation Desert Storm. The study analyzes the forces involved, the mining conducted, and the impact of mining and mine countermeasures on achieving surprise in the assault. It concludes that sufficient force levels are crucial for successful amphibious assaults and emphasizes the importance of rapid and complete mine countermeasures to achieve surprise. The document provides historical context, discusses strategic and operational considerations in amphibious warfare, and highlights the significance of mine warfare in amphibious operations.

ACTION ITEMS

Further research on the specific effects of sea mining on amphibious warfare, including more case studies and analysis of other conflicts.

Conduct a comparative analysis of different mine countermeasures techniques and their effectiveness in achieving surprise in amphibious assaults.

Explore the potential impact of new technologies and advancements in mine warfare on future amphibious operations.

Consider the implications of sea mining for naval strategy and force structure in amphibious warfare scenarios.

Investigate the role of intelligence gathering and reconnaissance in identifying and countering sea mines during amphibious assaults.

VIEWPOINTS

These perspectives increase the reader's exposure to viewpoint diversity.

GROUNDS FOR DISSENT

One possible reason for a member of the organization responsible for this document to dissent from the report is if they have principled concerns about the methodology used in the study. They may argue that the case studies selected are not representative enough to draw broad conclusions about the effects of sea mining on amphibious warfare. For example, they may argue that the inclusion of only four case studies does not provide a comprehensive enough analysis to make definitive claims.

Furthermore, they may question the criteria used to determine success in amphibious assaults. The report states that force levels are crucial for success, but a dissenting member may argue that there are other equally important factors, such as strategic planning, coordination with air and naval support, and intelligence gathering. They may contend that focusing solely on force levels oversimplifies the complexities of amphibious operations and fails to consider other important variables.

Another substantive reason for dissent could be a disagreement with the emphasis placed on mine countermeasures as a means to achieve surprise in amphibious assaults. A dissenting member might argue that surprise can be achieved through various other tactics and strategies, such as diversionary attacks, deception operations, or innovative approaches to landing techniques. They may believe that the report's heavy emphasis on mine countermeasures overlooks alternative methods to achieve surprise and limits creative thinking in future amphibious operations.

Moreover, a dissenting member might raise ethical concerns regarding sea mining itself. They may assert that the destructive nature of sea mines poses significant risks to civilian populations, marine life, and the environment. They could argue that this aspect was not adequately addressed in the report and should be given more consideration when evaluating the overall effectiveness of sea mining in amphibious warfare.

Overall, these hypothetical reasons for dissent stem from concerns about methodological limitations, oversimplification of complex factors, alternative approaches to achieving surprise, and ethical implications associated with sea mining. By raising these objections, the dissenting member aims to encourage a more comprehensive and nuanced understanding of the topic at hand.

RED TEAM CRITIQUE

Upon reviewing the document on the effects of sea mining on amphibious warfare, several key weaknesses and areas for improvement have been identified.

Firstly, while the document provides case studies of amphibious assaults conducted at Gallipoli, Normandy, Wonsan, and the Persian Gulf during Operation Desert Storm, it lacks a comprehensive analysis of other significant amphibious assaults throughout history. By limiting its focus to only these specific examples, it fails to capture a holistic understanding of the effects of sea mining on amphibious warfare. Including additional case studies or providing a rationale for why these specific ones were chosen would strengthen the research.

Additionally, the study's emphasis on force levels as crucial to successful amphibious assaults is oversimplified and lacks depth. While acknowledging that adequate force levels are important for success is valid, it fails to explore other factors such as mission planning, intelligence gathering capabilities or interagency coordination that may equally contribute to operational success in an amphibious assault context. The thesis should delve further into these aspects and provide a more nuanced perspective.

Furthermore, while discussing mine countermeasures' importance in achieving surprise in amphibious assaults is commendable within this document's scope; there should be more critical analysis regarding different techniques employed by opposing forces during case studies mentioned earlier. Understanding how they countered minefields deployed against them could provide valuable insights into potential strategies or tactics employed by enemy forces today.

The historical context provided by the document is limited to general strategic and operational considerations without delving deeper into specific technological advancements or changes over time that might affect contemporary mine warfare practices. Incorporating an examination of how technology has evolved since previous conflicts can offer both valuable lessons learned and potential challenges faced by modern-day naval forces in conducting successful amphibious operations amidst advanced mine countermeasures implemented by adversaries.

Finally, when discussing the significance of mine warfare in amphibious operations overall - focusing solely on its impact on achieving surprise overlooks other equally critical elements such as disruption of enemy logistics, denial of access, and area denial. A more comprehensive analysis that covers a range of strategic objectives and factors contributing to overall operational success would greatly enhance the document's value.

In conclusion, although this document provides valuable insights into the effects of sea mining on amphibious warfare, it is limited in scope and lacks critical analysis in several areas. By expanding case studies beyond the mentioned examples, exploring other factors influencing success beyond force levels alone, incorporating technological advancements over time within historical context, analyzing opponent strategies to mine countermeasures during specific case studies mentioned earlier will significantly strengthen this research's credibility and relevance.

MAGA Perspective

This document is just another example of liberal academia pushing their agenda and trying to undermine the greatness of America. The thesis focuses on sea mining, a tactic used by our enemies, as if it's some kind of noble strategy that we should be concerned about. Instead of promoting American exceptionalism and our military strength, this document seems to be siding with those who wish to harm us.

By analyzing amphibious assaults conducted at Gallipoli, Normandy, Wonsan, and the Persian Gulf, the author is clearly cherry-picking examples that fit their narrative. They conveniently ignore countless successful amphibious operations throughout history that did not involve sea mining. This selective approach only serves to distort the truth and push an anti-American agenda.

The idea that force levels are crucial for the success of amphibious assaults is an obvious statement that doesn't require a whole thesis to prove. Of course having adequate force levels will lead to successful operations. But what this document fails to acknowledge is the unparalleled strength and firepower of the United States military. Our armed forces have proven time and again that they can overcome any obstacle, including sea mining, with sheer determination and innovation.

Furthermore, emphasizing the importance of mine countermeasures in achieving surprise in amphibious assaults just shows how out of touch this document is with reality. Surprise should not be reliant on countering enemy tactics; instead, our military should aim to completely overwhelm and overpower our adversaries. We don't need sneaky methods like mine countermeasures when we can simply dominate the battlefield through superior force.

In conclusion, this document is yet another attempt by left-leaning academics to undermine American military prowess. It ignores historical context and selectively chooses examples that support its biased viewpoint. As patriotic Americans, we should reject such divisive narratives and focus on celebrating the strength and superiority of our great nation.

Page-by-Page Summaries

BODY-2 — LCDR James F. Ball's thesis on the effects of sea mining on amphibious warfare is approved by the thesis committee and accepted by the director of graduate degree programs. The opinions expressed are those of the student author and do not necessarily represent the views of the U.S. Army Command and General Staff College or any government agency.

BODY-3 — This study examines the effects of sea mining on amphibious warfare through case studies of past assaults. It determines that force levels are the determining factor for success, emphasizing the importance of rapid and complete mine countermeasures. A recommendation to prevent deterioration of countermeasures is presented.

BODY-4 — Acknowledgements for the assistance and support provided by various individuals and organizations in the field of mine warfare.

BODY-5 — The page contains a table of contents for a document that includes an introduction, literature review, case studies in mine warfare, conclusions and recommendations, and an appendix.

BODY-6 — The page provides a list of figures related to various mining and submarine campaigns in World War II, the Russo-Japanese War, and World War I. It also includes information on German influence mines, minesweeper losses, Gallipoli shore batteries, and minesweepers in commission from 1946-1953.

BODY-7 — The U.S. Navy's ability to conduct timely mine clearance operations has significantly decreased, making large-scale amphibious operations difficult and tactically unfeasible. Mining is a cost-effective form of naval warfare that presents a constant threat to enemy vessels, regardless of weather conditions. Mining can be defensive or offensive and requires valuable resources and time.

BODY-8 — Advancements in mine technology have made them more sophisticated, with options to upgrade older mines with modern electronics and sensors. The Manta mine, made by Misar S.p.A., is an example of a sophisticated anti-landing mine.

BODY-9 — Manta and Bofors GMI 100 Rockan are underwater mines with long operational lives. Mine countermeasures technology has not advanced significantly, as mines are still cleared in a similar manner to World War II. Influence mines are harder to clear than magnetically fuzed mines.

BODY-10 — The page discusses various techniques and advancements in mine clearance, including electrical current, acoustic sweeping, magnetic field reduction, and modern counter-sweep devices. Mines now have variable arming delays and non-ferrous materials to make detection more difficult.

BODY-11 — Integrated circuit technology has allowed the development of small memory devices for mines, enabling them to be programmed for specific targets. The costs of mining and submarine campaigns are also mentioned.

BODY-12 — Mines are widely available and sold to countries that can afford them, with Italy being a major manufacturer. Companies like Bofors A.G. and BAE aggressively market sophisticated mines, while others offer upgrades for existing arsenals. Basic mines can also be manufactured by countries with weapons industries.

BODY-13 — Mines are cost-effective, easy to use, and possess a devastating impact. They require significant countermeasures and have been proven effective in causing damage to naval vessels.

BODY-14 — The page discusses the threat of mines to naval operations, particularly in amphibious warfare. It raises questions about the feasibility of large-scale *amphibious operations and the level of losses and mine clearance effort that can be expected.*

BODY-15 *This page discusses the potential challenges and concerns related to mine clearance for amphibious operations, including the duration of sweep efforts, enemy awareness, expected losses, effectiveness of current forces, adequacy of minesweeping techniques, impact of mine technology, and the importance of the amphibious option in the strategic environment.*

BODY-16 *The page discusses the relationship between the likelihood of achieving surprise in an amphibious assault and the amount of time devoted to mine clearance. It also provides definitions for various terms related to amphibious operations.*

BODY-17 *This page provides definitions and descriptions of various terms related to amphibious operations, including sea echelon, transport area, fire support area, line of departure, boat lane, assault echelon, and assault follow on echelons.*

BODY-18 *This page provides definitions for key terms related to amphibious operations, including the roles of commanders, landing areas, landing sites, and landing craft.*

BODY-19 *This page provides definitions and explanations of various terms related to naval mines, including different types of mines, minefields, and techniques for locating and disposing of mines.*

BODY-20 *This page discusses different types of mines and their effects on amphibious operations. It emphasizes the importance of maintaining mine countermeasures capability to ensure the viability of large-scale surface amphibious assaults.*

BODY-21 *During the Civil War and Russo-Japanese War, mines caused significant losses for the Union Navy and Japanese Army respectively. Mines were used strategically to deter enemy forces and resulted in the sinking of several ships.*

BODY-22 *Mines played a significant role in World War I, particularly during the Gallipoli operation and the North Sea Barrage. They sank ships, restricted movement, and hindered Allied forces, leading to the withdrawal of troops and impacting amphibious warfare.*

BODY-23 *During World War I, approximately 205,000 mines were laid resulting in the loss of 63 Allied and 60 Central Powers warships. In World War II, there were mining campaigns conducted by both the Germans and Americans against their respective enemies.*

BODY-24 *During World War II, the Germans heavily mined British waters and initiated attacks on coastal traffic off the U.S. Eastern Seaboard using submarines and aircraft as mine layers. They introduced magnetic, acoustic, and pressure fuzing to mine warfare.*

BODY-25 *The page discusses the effectiveness of German influence mines in causing significant damage to ships, particularly in shallow water. These mines had different fuzing mechanisms and were primarily magnetic or acoustic in nature.*

BODY-26 *During World War II, the British used commercial fishing boats as minesweepers to combat the Royal Navy. German technology forced the British to develop new minesweeping methods. The Germans constructed defensive and offensive minefields along the French coast in preparation for an amphibious assault.*

BODY-27 *Germans heavily mined the Seine Bay to prevent invasion, but the Allies successfully swept the mines in 24 hours, maintaining surprise. The early recognition of the threat and commitment of resources contributed to the success at Normandy. Sixteen ships were still lost during the operation.*

BODY-28 The Germans designed complex mine fields in Normandy, but disagreements between the Army and Navy prevented their full implementation. The United States successfully used mines against Japan, causing significant losses to their naval and merchant fleets. Japan had no effective minesweeping capability.

BODY-29 The page discusses the strategic mining campaign conducted by Allied Forces during World War II, which effectively blockaded Japan and damaged their merchant marine. The use of mines by American forces resulted in losses for both enemy and friendly ships.

BODY-30 The page provides statistics on the losses of minesweepers in World War I, broken down by country and region.

BODY-31 World War II saw advancements in mine warfare, including the German influence fuze and British development of magnetic and acoustic sweeps. The Allies also introduced airborne mine countermeasures.

BODY-32 After World War II, the US Navy's mine warfare capabilities were greatly reduced. Mine warfare was considered an unglamorous and career-damaging field. Hyman Rickover and the University of California at San Diego made important contributions to mine hunting technology.

BODY-33 The Navy's focus on nuclear weapons and high-performance aircraft after World War II led to a decline in mine warfare forces. However, the Korean War highlighted the importance of mines as a cost-effective weapon. The Navy encountered heavy mining at Wonsan during an amphibious operation, causing delays and frustration.

BODY-34 During the Korean War, mines caused significant delays and casualties for the United Nations forces. The use of mines by North Koreans led to an expansion of the mine warfare force and experimentation with countermeasures such as aircraft and combat swimmers.

BODY-35 After the Korean War, the Navy expanded its mine force but faced little challenge in Vietnam. They used mines to close Haiphong harbor and conducted a large-scale mine clearance operation called Operation End Sweep. After the war, the Navy underwent a drawdown and focused on developing airborne options for mine clearance.

BODY-36 The Iran-Iraq war in the 1980s involved both sides using mines in the Persian Gulf. The United States entered the conflict after one of its ships was damaged, leading to a mine countermeasures force being deployed. However, the Iranians continued to mine until the war ended in 1988.

BODY-37 The mine countermeasures force returned to the Persian Gulf due to increased US naval presence and the threat of amphibious assault. Iraq heavily mined the northern reaches of the Gulf, posing a risk to ships and personnel. The minesweeping force cleared over 1600 mines by September 1991.

BODY-38 The study examines the potential consequences of neglecting mine countermeasures forces, which could hinder amphibious assaults and compromise military operations in the Persian Gulf due to residual mines.

BODY-39 The literature on mine warfare is divided into tactical and technical branches, with limited primary source material available. The volume of literature corresponds to the level of interest at different times, with spikes after major conflicts. There are few books specifically focused on amphibious aspects of mining.

BODY-40 This page provides information on various publications about mine warfare, including a technical history, a history of American contribution, and a summary *history. It also mentions a publication about General Erwin Rommel's preparation for the Allied invasion in Normandy.*

BODY-41 *The page discusses the coverage of various military operations in literature, including Gallipoli, Normandy, Korean operations, and Operation Desert Storm. It mentions that the information on these operations can be contradictory and at variance with the facts.*

BODY-42 *Various sources, including trade journals and military periodicals, provide comprehensive data and analysis on mine warfare, with a focus on force size, composition, technical details, historical events, and tactical insights. European navies show a consistent commitment to mine warfare compared to the cyclical swings of the USN.*

BODY-43 *This page discusses the content of professional journals on mine warfare, written by naval officers with experience in the field. The articles provide insight into tactical and technical knowledge during different periods of significant mining activity. The early works focus on technical characteristics and practical difficulties, while later articles serve as "lessons learned."*

BODY-44 *Sea Barrage is missing from the literature, but interest in mine warfare increased after World War II. The success of Operations Starvation and Paukenshlag led to insightful articles on the topic in Proceedings from 1945-1950.*

BODY-45 *The page discusses the challenges of dealing with sea mines during World War II, particularly in the Pacific theater. It highlights the need to clear friendly minefields before reaching beaches and emphasizes the difficulty of clearing land mines on beaches and in shallow waters. The use of combat swimmers and small minesweeping boats close to the beach is mentioned as a possible solution.*

BODY-46 *The page discusses the history of mine warfare in the Korean War and Vietnam War, highlighting the initial failures and subsequent improvements in organizing and training assault minesweeping elements. It also mentions the use of helicopters as a mine warfare asset.*

BODY-47 *The page discusses various military operations and literature related to them, including the clearance of the Suez Canal and experiences in the Persian Gulf. It also mentions primary sources such as evaluation reports from the Commander in Chief of the U.S. Pacific Fleet during the Korean War.*

BODY-48 *The page discusses the use of doctrinal publications in research, specifically JCS Publication 3-02 and the Naval Warfare Publication series. These publications provide amphibious and mine warfare doctrine for the Navy and Marine Corps.*

BODY-49 *This chapter discusses the methods and procedures for the thesis, which will analyze historical data and compare it to current conditions. It will examine four major operations and the effect of mining and mine countermeasures on each. The study will also consider changing technology.*

BODY-50 *The page discusses the relationship between surprise, clearance time, and force totals in minefield clearance. It aims to determine if the number of sweep assets or level of technology is more important in clearing minefields quickly. Historical data and interviews with experienced officers will be used to analyze the topic.*

BODY-51 *Amphibious warfare is a powerful tool for military strategists, allowing for surprise attacks and potentially changing the course of a war. The nautical phase is not affected by terrain and offers few restrictions to movement. Any nation with a coastline is vulnerable to amphibious invasion.*

BODY-52 Amphibious warfare is flexible but vulnerable. Success depends on quickly building up military strength on the beach before the enemy can react. Attacks should be made in lightly defended areas and isolation of defenders is necessary. Extensive fire support is required from ships and aircraft until landing forces establish their own support means.

BODY-53 Amphibious assaults are sensitive to disruptions in timing and synchronization, which can severely disrupt assault momentum. Despite this, amphibious operations continue to be favored by planners due to their potential for high rewards or disastrous consequences. Minefields can be used by defenders to limit the threat and make it more predictable.

BODY-54 Mines can provide cost-effective protection against sea attacks, but breaching them takes time and allows the enemy to analyze and defend against the assault. Four case studies will explore the impact of mines on amphibious assaults.

BODY-55 Gallipoli was a failed amphibious warfare operation during World War I, resulting in the loss of over half a million men. The operation's failure was largely due to a lack of surprise caused by less than 500 mines. Turkey's entry into the war on the side of the Central Powers was not assured and they were ill-prepared to fight against Great Britain and France.

BODY-56 The page discusses the decline of the Ottoman Empire and its strategic importance due to its geographical location.

BODY-57 The page discusses the failed alliance between Turkey and the Central Powers due to British interference with the delivery of battleships. The Turks ultimately signed an alliance with Germany but did not follow through on their commitments.

BODY-58 German warships SMS Goeben and SMS Breslau shell Algerian ports, evade Royal Navy, enter Dardanelles, commissioned into Turkish Navy. Attack Russian ports without Turkish government's approval, leading to war declaration by Russia, France, and Great Britain.

BODY-59 Turkey's military was in no condition to fight, but with the help of the German Military Mission, they were able to maintain order and challenge the great powers of Europe. There were a few incidents during October-December, including expeditions and shelling of forts.

BODY-60 The British consider a naval assault on Istanbul to relieve pressure on the Russians and divert German forces from the Western Front, but some are reluctant due to concerns about resources.

BODY-61 The page discusses the plan to force the straits of Istanbul during World War I, led by Winston Churchill and Admiral Fisher. They proposed using obsolete battleships to bombard the city and destroy its forts. Vice Admiral Sackville-Carden was tasked with preparing the plan.

BODY-62 The page discusses the force requirements and plan for the naval attacks on the Dardanelles during World War I, with the goal of demolishing Turkish forts. The plan was approved by the Admiralty and involved battleships, cruisers, destroyers, submarines, seaplanes, and minesweepers.

BODY-63 The page describes the strategic importance of the Narrows in controlling the Dardanelles, with details about the fortifications and armaments in place, including mines laid to slow down ships.

BODY-64 Allied forces attacked the forts guarding the Dardanelles entrance in 1915, but were not completely successful due to inaccurate long-range firing and lack of continuous aiming fire control systems.

BODY-65 The page discusses the decision to engage forts with direct fire, the successful attack on the forts by Vice Admiral De Robeck, and the challenges faced by the mine sweeping force.

BODY-66 The minesweepers at Gallipoli faced a dilemma as they couldn't remove the mines until the guns were suppressed, and the guns couldn't be suppressed until the mines were swept. The crews felt overwhelmed and frustrated by the constant gunfire. Despite attempts to sweep the mines, they failed due to enemy fire.

BODY-67 Minesweepers were not successful in their task and suffered heavy casualties, but the Admiralty considered them expendable. Churchill expressed a willingness to accept casualties in order to complete the mission. The Allied fleet prepared for a full-scale assault on the straits.

BODY-68 British and French battleships bombard Turkish forts at Chanak and Kilid Bahr, with the French suffering a loss when the battleship Bouvet strikes a mine and sinks. Turkish fire is silenced by 4:00 p.m.

BODY-69 The Allies suffered heavy losses in the Dardanelles when their ships struck mines laid by Lieutenant Colonel Geehl, a Turkish defense expert. The minesweepers only found three of the twenty mines laid, and aerial reconnaissance failed to detect them.

BODY-70 The page discusses the events surrounding General Sir Ian Hamilton's role in the Gallipoli expedition and Admiral Keyes' reorganization of the minesweeping fleet. The answer to why Keyes didn't use his superior force is not provided.

BODY-71 The Allies' plan to open the straits and capture Istanbul during the Gallipoli campaign was compromised, losing the element of surprise. It became a race between the Allies and the Turks to fortify and assemble combat power ashore.

BODY-72 The Gallipoli campaign in 1916 saw Allied forces struggle to advance on the peninsula due to Turkish defenders and naval limitations. Plans to attack from the rear were hindered by protected minefields, preventing a breakthrough.

BODY-73 The evacuation of the Allied forces from the Gallipoli peninsula in 1916 resulted in high casualties due to the effective mine warfare efforts of the Turkish Army. Technological factors, such as the use of moored contact mines and inadequate sweep gear, contributed to the failure of the operation.

BODY-74 The failure of mine clearance, inadequate training, and lack of nerve by the senior commander led to the tragedy of Gallipoli. The loss of tactical surprise makes a large-scale amphibious assault unfeasible.

BODY-75 The page discusses the minesweeping efforts and naval assault on the Narrows during the Gallipoli campaign, indicating that an amphibious assault was forthcoming. It also mentions the level of losses suffered by amphibious forces entering a mined area and the level of mine clearance effort required for a large-scale assault. The sweep effort alerted the enemy to a probable landing but did not reveal the exact beach location.

BODY-76 The page discusses the expected losses and effectiveness of mine clearance forces during an amphibious assault. It concludes that despite significant losses to minesweepers, the force would still be combat effective due to the large number of ships used and the spacing between mines.

BODY-77 Current minesweeping techniques, specifically the use of paravanes, were effective in clearing an amphibious operation area. The technology of the mines did not significantly impact the duration of the minesweeping operation at Gallipoli.

BODY-78 World War I taught valuable lessons in mine warfare, leading to the development of more sophisticated devices like magnetically actuated mines. These mines are complex and sensitive to various influences, making them harder to detect and disarm.

BODY-79   The page discusses the development of minesweeping techniques and new minesweepers in the United States and the Royal Navy during World War II.

BODY-80   The page discusses the development and acquisition of minesweepers by the United States Navy during World War II, including the Raven class fleet minesweeper and the use of commercial fishing boats as coastal minesweepers.

BODY-81   The page discusses the advancements in mine warfare during World War I, including the design of the yard motor minesweeper and the accumulation of knowledge in mine clearance operations. However, after the war, there was a lack of interest and neglect in mine warfare by major navies.

BODY-82   During World War II, the British and Germans engaged in intense mine warfare. The Germans had a stock of 200,000 mines and began laying them as soon as the war started. The British responded by requisitioning ships for minesweeping operations. Both sides developed new weapons and countermeasures throughout the war.

BODY-83   Unexplained explosions and sinking of ships reported along the coast, attributed to magnetic mines. British developed countermeasures including a large magnetic coil on a barge and airborne mine countermeasures using Wellington bombers. Premature explosions remained a problem.

BODY-84   The page discusses the development and use of magnetic field generators in trawlers for mine sweeping during World War II. It also mentions the construction of wooden hulled vessels and the techniques of de-perming and degaussing to reduce a ship's magnetic field.

BODY-85   The page discusses the tactics and adaptations used by the Royal Navy to sweep and neutralize different types of mines during World War II, including magnetic, moored contact, and acoustically actuated mines. It also mentions the countermeasures developed to sweep the acoustically actuated mines.

BODY-86   During World War II, the British Commonwealth Navies used specialized equipment to sweep and neutralize magnetic, acoustic, and contact mines. They experienced losses but were able to adapt and increase their minecraft fleet. The Germans introduced more sophisticated mines that were harder to sweep.

BODY-87   The page discusses the development of acoustic mines and the adoption of British countermeasures techniques by the US Navy during World War II.

BODY-88   The page discusses the training of the fleet to recover lost skills, the German U-Boat campaign off the US East coast, and the efforts to clear mines.

BODY-89   In 1943, the mine warfare forces had a quiet year with reduced mine counts and losses. They were able to focus on shipbuilding and prepare for their first major amphibious assault, Operation Husky. The invasion was supported by a task force of ships and minesweepers. Operation Avalanche, the invasion of the Italian mainland at Salerno, was also supported by minesweepers.

BODY-90   Assault sweeping techniques were successfully used to clear mines during an amphibious assault, validating their effectiveness. The process involved a sequence of fast clearance by large minesweepers, followed by smaller boats and divers clearing closer to the shore.

BODY-91   The page discusses the use of minesweepers in European assaults during World War II, particularly in Operation Overlord. It also mentions General Rommel's use of sea mines as part of his obstacle system to prevent amphibious assaults.

BODY-92 The page discusses the German minelaying campaign during a naval assault, including their strategic use of different types of mines and sweep obstructors. The effectiveness of the campaign was hindered by internal politics and a lack of maximum mine laying.

BODY-93 Allies executed a large and complex minesweeping operation for Operation Overlord, fooling the Germans into not laying planned mine defenses. A fleet of 385 minesweepers, mostly British and Canadian, cleared channels across the English Channel and prepared for the invasion.

BODY-95 Minesweepers cleared channels for invasion force, only one ship lost. Minesweepers observed but not reported by Germans. Minesweepers engaged by shore batteries near coast.

BODY-96 The success of the D-Day invasion in 1944 can be attributed to the efficient and experienced minesweeping forces, who cleared a large area for the assault and surprised the Germans. Without their expertise, the invasion would not have been possible.

BODY-97 The page discusses the impact of mine casualties on naval forces during World War II and the prevention of German use of a new undersea weapon called the "oyster" mine during the Allied invasion.

BODY-98 Speed restrictions during the Normandy invasion disrupted timing and synchronization, potentially hindering the buildup of the beachhead and logistics movement. However, the initial surprise prevented the Germans from using their unsweepable mines until later stages of the assault.

BODY-99 The page discusses the clearing of mines during the Normandy operation, with the British losing 14 ships and the Americans losing 34 ships. The loss of tactical surprise made a large-scale amphibious operation unfeasible, and the expected level of losses for amphibious forces entering a mined area was one ship per 28.2 mines cleared.

BODY-100 The page discusses the level of mine clearance effort required for a large-scale amphibious assault, using Utah Beach as an example. It states that 85 minesweepers were needed for the pre-assault sweep and three months of continued clearance. In 1991, with 28 minecraft available, it would take three days to conduct the assault sweeping portion alone. The historical loss rate at Normandy was 2.28%, with seven minecraft lost. If this loss rate is applied to current force levels

BODY-101 Current minesweeping techniques are adequate to clear an amphibious operating area in a timely manner, as demonstrated by the techniques used at Normandy. Lessons from Normandy include the importance of numbers, the role of mine technology, and the significance of experience and training.

BODY-102 After World War II, the US and its Allies reduced their naval forces, resulting in the loss of over 500 mine warfare ships and thousands of officers and enlisted men. The primary task became clearing the mines laid in Japanese waters, which was completed by February 1946.

BODY-103 The page discusses the decline in training and readiness of the American minesweeper force after the disestablishment of a command responsible for developing plans and enforcing standards. It also mentions the Soviets' extensive mining operations and their potential assistance to North Korea in combatting sea power.

BODY-104 The Soviets analyzed the Korean coastline and found that the west coast was not suitable for mining or amphibious operations, while the east coast was ideal. The North Koreans invaded with Soviet support, pushing South Korean forces back. The

US reinforced them but were defeated. To break the siege, General Macarthur conducted an amphibious assault at Inchon called Operation Chromite.

BODY-105 The page discusses the successful Inchon landing and its impact on the collapse of North Korean resistance, leading to the recapture of Seoul and pursuit of the North Korean army. It also mentions General Macarthur's plan for an amphibious assault on the east coast at Wonsan.

BODY-106 The page discusses a military plan to trap North Korean elements by linking up two armies at Pyongyang, with an amphibious assault on Wonsan using the 1st Marine Division and the 7th Infantry Division.

BODY-107 Admiral C. Turner Joy issued a directive to Vice Admiral Arthur D. Struble, outlining missions for the amphibious task force including maintaining a blockade, providing support to the Eighth Army, conducting pre D-Day operations, loading and transporting X Corps, seizing a beachhead in Wonsan, and providing initial support to X Corps at Wonsan. The document also warned of possible mines in the area.

BODY-108 The amphibious task force sailed to the objective, but the operation was no longer necessary as North Korean resistance had deteriorated. The decision was made to land the X Corps at Wonsan in an administrative rather than tactical operation. Minesweeping preparations were successful.

BODY-109 The USS Rochester encountered additional moored mines obstructing the beach. Captain Spofford attempted brute force minesweeping, but it was unsuccessful. The minefield had been laid by Koreans under Soviet supervision, with delayed action magnetic mines also planted. Mechanical minesweeping resumed later on.

BODY-110 During a military operation, two ships struck mines and sank. A conservative approach was then taken to clear the area using helicopters, flying boats, and divers. A channel was eventually cleared in five days, but a Korean minesweeper was destroyed by a Soviet magnetic mine. Around 3000 mines had been laid in total.

BODY-111 The landing at Wonsan during the Korean War shocked the Navy and led to the development of non-magnetic minesweepers. The tactical loss was insignificant, but it highlighted the potential dangers of delays offshore.

BODY-112 The page discusses the feasibility of a large-scale amphibious assault, considering factors such as loss of tactical surprise, casualties from entering mined areas, and the level of mine clearance effort required. It concludes that the available forces would require approximately 6.5 days to conduct the operation.

BODY-113 The enemy had already identified potential landing areas. The sweep effort confirmed these areas and engaged enemy shore batteries. Historical data shows a 11.5% loss of minesweepers, but this would not render an amphibious assault force combat ineffective. Current minesweeping techniques are adequate for timely clearance in the given environment.

BODY-114 The page discusses the use of new technologies and strategies in mine countermeasures during the Korean War, specifically focusing on the operation at Wonsan. It highlights the importance of intelligence and numbers in achieving successful mine clearance operations.

BODY-115 The page discusses the challenges faced during the Wonsan operation, highlighting the importance of mines in naval warfare and the need for effective amphibious forces. As a result, the US Navy planned to add over 150 minecraft to its fleet by 1960.

BODY-116 The decline of wooden minesweepers in the 1960s and 70s due to advancements in nuclear submarines and aircraft carriers. Helicopters were introduced for airborne *minesweeping, reducing the need for surface minesweeping. Lack of resources and attention caused the minesweeping force to shrink.*

BODY-117 *During the 1980s, the US Navy's mine countermeasures force significantly decreased while European members of NATO advanced in mine warfare tactics and technology. The US relied on Europe for mine countermeasures due to military strategy, with the US Navy focusing on strike power projection against the Soviet Union.*

BODY-118 *During the Iran-Iraq war, both sides attempted to use mines in their naval warfare but were unsuccessful due to lack of intelligence analysis and technical errors.*

BODY-119 *During the Iran-Iraq war, both sides attacked merchant shipping in the Persian Gulf. Kuwait sought assistance to protect its oil ports by placing its tankers under American, British, and Soviet flags. The Iranians retaliated with mining, prompting a response from the US and other nations.*

BODY-120 *Ships were sent to the Persian Gulf to sweep for mines, but continued to strike them. Mining ceased after engagements with the US Navy and a multinational force completed the operation in 1990. Following the invasion of Kuwait, an amphibious task force and mine countermeasures forces were deployed.*

BODY-121 *After a training exercise, floating mines appeared in the Saudi oil field of Saffiniyeh. These mines were recently laid and of a new design, causing concern as there were no effective countermeasures.*

BODY-122 *During the Persian Gulf War, mines in the northern Persian Gulf posed a threat to naval forces. The location of the minefields was unknown, making surveillance impossible. Despite efforts to analyze hydrographic conditions, no minefields were encountered. Naval gunfire support was needed for ground operations, requiring a cleared channel for battleships Missouri and Wisconsin.*

BODY-123 *The page discusses the need for mine countermeasures support during a landing operation conducted by an amphibious task force. Despite limited resources, minesweeping operations were initiated but were interrupted when one of the ships struck a moored contact mine.*

BODY-124 *The page discusses a ship that was damaged by a mine explosion and the efforts to clear minefields in order to allow battleships access to their firing positions. The potential casualties from mines are mentioned.*

BODY-125 *The page discusses the challenges and methods of minesweeping after a cease-fire in Iraq, including the use of magnetic sweeping equipment and the discovery of maldeployed mines.*

BODY-126 *The page discusses the failure to recognize and address the threat of Iraqi mine warfare in the Persian Gulf during Desert Storm, despite previous knowledge and experience.*

BODY-127 *Large scale amphibious assault was deemed feasible due to the use of amphibious forces as a deception and the swift victory by ground forces. Historical data suggests a potential loss of 6-10 ships (19%-32% of total force) when entering a mined area. With available assets in 1991, it would have taken four to six days to clear an amphibious operating area for such an assault.*

BODY-128 *The page discusses the potential alerting of enemies during a sweep effort, historical data on mine clearance losses, and the effectiveness of current minesweeping techniques in clearing an amphibious operating area.*

BODY-129 *The page discusses the impact of different mine technologies on mine sweeping operations and the potential loss of large-scale amphibious assaults. It also mentions the decline of mine warfare and future plans for mine countermeasures ships.*

BODY-131 High technology sea mines in Gallipoli eliminated tactical surprise, while in Normandy they did not. The mines in Normandy were state of the art but did not delay the assault and their effect was not critical.

BODY-132 The page discusses the importance of tactical surprise in large-scale amphibious operations, using examples such as Gallipoli and Normandy. It also mentions how modern surveillance systems make it difficult to conceal minesweeping activity off an enemy coast.

BODY-133 The page discusses the level of losses expected by amphibious forces entering a mined area and the effort required to sweep an amphibious operating area. It also mentions the duration of a sweep effort and whether it would alert the enemy to potential landing areas.

BODY-134 The page discusses historical data on mine clearance operations in various military campaigns and concludes that losses from mines would not render a modern amphibious task force combat ineffective. The effectiveness of minesweeping techniques depends on training and availability of forces, rather than the technology itself.

BODY-135 The page discusses the impact of mine technology on amphibious assaults, highlighting the importance of minesweeping and the potential consequences of failure. It concludes that current tactics are adequate but clearance times can be lengthy, and more forces are needed for rapid sweeps. The probability of success decreases without surprise and isolation of a beachhead.

BODY-136 The proliferation of high technology sea mines has reduced surprise in amphibious assaults, with force composition and training being key factors. Further study is recommended to design a mine countermeasures force capable of clearing a large area quickly and to improve readiness and training standards.

BODY-138 List of landing craft and destroyers involved in the Normandy invasion on June 6.

BODY-141 A list of books on various topics including World War II, the Korean War, and naval history.

BODY-142 A list of articles on naval mines and mine warfare from various sources.

NOTABLE PASSAGES

BODY-3   *"The study attempts to determine if the determining factor is the level of mine technology, the level of countermeasures technology, or the size of the forces committed. It emphasizes the importance of rapid and complete mine countermeasures to the achievement of surprise in the amphibious assault."*

BODY-7   *"Of all the forms of naval warfare, mining is arguably the most cost effective. A well conceived and properly laid minefield presents a constant and serious threat to enemy vessels and is minimally affected by weather or environmental conditions. It may be planned to suit a variety of operational scenarios. It may be defensive, designed to protect friendly ports or coastal areas, or it may be offensive, designed to attack the enemy in his harbors and deny him the use of the sea."*

BODY-8   *"There has been a quantum leap in the sophistication of the mine, and a number of mine manufacturers are offering to upgrade older mines with modern electronics and sensors."*

BODY-9   *"There has not been a corresponding quantum leap in mine countermeasures technology. With some changes, mines are still cleared much the same way they were cleared during World War II."*

BODY-10   *"The magnetic sweeping, acoustic sweeping, and magnetic field reduction techniques were developed by the British during World War II in response to German mining operations."*

BODY-11   *"Finally, integrated circuit technology has allowed the development of small memory devices for mines which allow the mines to be programmed for specific targets while ignoring others."*

BODY-12   *"Mines are proliferating. The sea mine is viewed as a purely defensive weapon by the majority of the world. As such, there are little restrictions on their sale and mines are generally made available to any country which can afford them."*

BODY-13   *"They are cheap, reasonably simple. reliable. producible in great numbers. easily stockpiled. and possess a devastating wallop. They require countermeasures which demand a great investment in forces and technology. For those who wage naval war, these are virtues to esteem. In pounds of explosive per dollar they are naval warfare's greatest bargain".*

BODY-14   *"The increasing sophistication of mines, their proliferation, and the decrease in mine countermeasure forces may have rendered such surprise unattainable."*

BODY-16   *"That the likelihood of achieving surprise in an amphibious assault is inversely proportional to the amount of time devoted to mine clearance."*

BODY-20   *"This study shall be significant in that it will serve to draw attention to the potential loss of a powerful tool of power projection. the amphibious assault. The Navy must once again be made aware of the unique vulnerability of large scale surface amphibious assaults to mine warfare and must make every effort to ensure that mine countermeasures capability does not deteriorate past the point that a rapid assault through a mined area is no longer possible."*

BODY-21   During the Russo-Japanese War both sides employed mines liberally. The Russians used mines extensively during the siege of Port Arthur, specifically to deter a landing by the Japanese Army. The Japanese lost eleven ships, including two battleships, to Russian mines and were forced to take the base by siege from landward.

BODY-22   *"The Allies were forced to retreat and the decision was made to take Istanbul by amphibious assault via the Gallipoli peninsula. The Turks employed controlled mines in connection with other obstacles to canalize the allied landing efforts. The minefields restricted the area available for fire support, assault, and resupply shipping. They also prevented Allied naval forces from interdicting the lines of communication extending from Istanbul to the Gallipoli Peninsula, allowing Axis forces unrestricted resupply and reinforcement."*

BODY-23 *"Approximately 205,000 mines were laid in World War I, resulting in the loss of 63 Allied and 60 Central Powers warships."*

BODY-24 *"The Germans inaugurated the use of submarines and aircraft as mine layers, and introduced magnetic, acoustic, and pressure fuzing to the world of mine warfare."*

BODY-26 *"German technology forced the British to develop magnetic and acoustic minesweeping methods which are still in use today."*

BODY-27 *"We have got to lay mines and still more mines in the Seine Bay with the tenacity of a bulldog. It is incomparably more effective to sink a whole cargo at sea than to have to fight the unloaded material and personnel on land."*

BODY-28 *"The Germans gave considerable thought to the defensive mine fields surrounding Normandy. designing complicated mixed-type fields covered by large caliber coastal artillery. Recognizing that fields in shallow water are particularly difficult to sweep they developed a series of shallow water mines designed to destroy landing craft."*

BODY-31 *"World War II served as the genesis of a number of technological advance in mine warfare. Already mentioned is the German development of the influence fuze in its various permutations. an innovation rapidly copied by the allies. The British developed and fielded a number of minesweeping devices. the first magnetic and acoustic sweeps. and by placing large magnetic coils in a Wellington bomber and flying at wavetop height they introduced the first airborne mine countermeasures."*

BODY-32 *"Perhaps most critically, particularly in peacetime, it is a career swamp. Senior officers ordered to duty in the mine forces have had the kiss of death laid on their careers. One First Lord of the British Admiralty summarized the prevalent attitude with the following comment. '... unpleasant work for a naval officer, an occupation like rat catching'."*

BODY-33 *"The North Koreans had no effective naval capability against the USN. which ranged freely along the Korean coast. projecting power inland via naval air and long-range gunnery. They discovered, with the help of their Soviet mentors, that the naval mine is a poor man's friend, a weapon whose effect is extremely disproportionate to its cost."*

BODY-34 *"We have lost control of the seas to a nation without a navy. using pre World War One weapons. laid by vessels which were utilized at the time of the birth of Christ."*

BODY-35 *"After the lessons of the Korean War the Navy greatly expanded the mine force and when Vietnam arrived they were ready for a challenge that failed to materialize. Some isolated incidents occurred, primarily in port areas, and largely as a result of direct actions by combat swimmers. Such operations, when encountered, were dealt with by naval special operations forces."*

BODY-36 *"The advent of the Iran-Iraq war in 1980 found both antagonists well equipped with mines and willing to use them. The Persian Gulf is arguably one of the most mineable bodies of water in the world. It is shallow, not exceeding 200 feet of depth across most of its expanse and it is sharply compartmented by shallows, oil fields, and various other unnavigable areas."*

BODY-37 Had an assault been required the amphibious task force would have been forced into incompletely swept water. placing 31 ships and over 30.000 personnel at severe risk.

BODY-38 "The significance of this study is to determine if we have possibly once again allowed our mine countermeasures forces to deteriorate to dangerous levels. and by doing so lost or severely compromised our ability to conduct major amphibious assaults in a timely manner."

BODY-41 "In almost every case all authors writing about Gallipoli understand the effects of the mines used there and cover them adnquatoly. Tho ontiro operation, from both military and naval aspects, is very well documented and easy to research."

BODY-42 "The depth and currency of this literature is sufficient to allow a reader to keep current with the pace of technology and provides a means to compare U.S. and European initiatives in the field."

BODY-43 "The articles in these professional journals provide a window into the depth of tactical and technical knowledge at the time. The earliest works are often quite lengthy and dwell on the technical characteristics of the mines, and the practical difficulties faced by the mariners who laid and swept them. World War One was the U.S. Navy's first great excursion into mine warfare and the immediate postwar literature of the early 1920's are simply 'lessons learned'. The Naval Institute Proceedings have often functioned as a public forum for such lessons, especially in earlier years when no official vehicle was in place for the promulgation of such information."

BODY-44 "After the end of World War II interest in mine warfare at all levels in the Navy appeared to accelerate. The experience of the thousands of sailors who were assigned minesweeping duties was reflected in the literature. For the first time the junior officers writing these articles began to attempt an analyses beyond the technical. The success of Operation Starvation and Operation Paukenshlag impressed the officers who were assigned to evaluate them and a number of superb articles are found in Proceedings from 1945-1950."

BODY-45 "The present day mine problem is one of the greatest headaches faced by future amphibious operations. From the four fathom line inward, experts are baffled by the problem at present but are undoubtedly seeking a solution. Unless we can completely isolate the landing areas the Pacific war style of mine clearance cannot be utilized."

BODY-46 "The need to organize and train assault minesweeping elements was again recognized. The first mention of the helicopter as a mine warfare asset is found in a 1951 article. Most importantly, the highest levels of the Navy became aware of the significance of the mine warfare threat."

BODY-47 "A significant primary source are the Commander in Chief, U.S. Pacific Fleet Interim Evaluation Reports for the Korean War. These documents, issued quarterly for the duration of the conflict, are divided into various naval warfare areas including mine and amphibious warfare. They evaluate the state of training, organization, staff adequacy, intelligence, planning, and tactics and techniques. Each provides an analysis of the successes and failures of that particular quarter including descriptions of operations and lessons learned. Conclusions are drawn based on the evidence and, where appropriate, recommendations are presented."

BODY-50 "Given the assumption that surprise is inversely proportional to the time devoted to mine countermeasures. I will then examine the timelines required for U.S. forces to clear a brigade sized amphibious operating area to determine if those times are excessive."

BODY-51 "Amphibious warfare, the sudden strike from the sea that surprises an enemy, upsets his plans, and potentially changes a war or campaign in a single stroke, has been a tool of military strategists since man first took to the water."

BODY-52 "The success of such an operation hinges upon a rapid buildup of military muscle on the beach. This must be done quickly, before an enemy can react and focus his forces against the beachhead."

BODY-53 "The true heart of naval warfare is the inherent mobility of the forces and the mine is the answer to that mobility. Minefields become the terrain of the nautical landscape, and can be used by the defender to impose parameters upon the amphibious threat. The minefields now become the 'No-Go' or 'Slo-Go' areas familiar to military staff officers, the gaps and lanes in the fields become avenues of approach, and suddenly the threat is considerably diminished and eminently more predictable."

BODY-54 "A nation which feels threatened by attack from the sea can achieve economies of force by employing mines. By establishing protective fields and focusing sensors and weapons systems upon these fields a good degree of protection can be achieved with relatively few forces. These fields are obstacles in the purest sense and must be breached by any force attempting to pass through them. As on land this breaching process takes time, that most critical and unrecoverable resource. The time spent in breaching a minefield will be used by an alert enemy to analyze the assault, mass forces for the defense, and if the beachhead cannot be isolated then the assault will likely fail."

BODY-55 "Gallipoli is to amphibious warfare what Cambrai is to the cavalryman, the first testing of modern techniques and equipment applied to an ancient problem. In the case of Gallipoli that test was to fail in the blood of over half a million men."

BODY-56 "For Turkey was cursed by geography to lie at the crossroads of empire. Occupying the northeastern Mediterranean littoral, and extending east to Iraq she sat athwart the major lines of communication between Britain and her empire, and controlled access to the Balkans via the Black Sea."

BODY-57 "The Turks had contracted and paid for two battleships. the Sultan Osman and the Reshadieh, to be built in British yards and delivered in the summer of 1914. The money, over thirty million dollars, had been raised by popular subscription from the Turkish population and tremendous national pride was invested in their acquisition. Using a variety of subterfuges, the British delayed the departure of the vessels from May until July. when Winston Churchill, as First Lord of the Admiralty, ordered them requisitioned. No compensation or repayment was offered."

BODY-58 "For three months the ships sat idle in the port of Istanbul, then, on October 28th the ships attacked the Russian ports of Odessa, Sevastopol, and Feodosiya. This attack was carried out without the sanction of the Turkish government, and they attempted to disavow it without success. On November 4th, Russia declared war on Turkey, followed the next day by France and Great Britain."

BODY-59 "The efforts of Enver Pasha and the 'Young Turks' notwithstanding. The Germans had established a military mission in 1913 to train the Turks. and had achieved considerable progress. Nevertheless, the series of Balkan Wars of independence prior to 1914 had drained and expended the Ottoman Army. Excepting only a few elite units, this army had gone unpaid for months, and some units were reportedly on the verge of mutiny. This army was barely ready to maintain order within its domains, and was not prepared to challenge the great powers of Europe."

BODY-60 "In Europe the trenches now extended from the North Sea to Switzerland. and the antagonists had already suffered over a million casualties. The British, long intrigued by the operational possibilities of a thrust into central Europe through the Balkans, began to reexamine some long discarded plans for a naval assault on Istanbul. This appeared to offer relief for the Russians, who had suffered from the

	disastrous battles at Tannenburg and the Masurian Lakes, would knock Turkey out of the war, and would divert German forces from the Western Front, thus offering some possibility for decisive action."
BODY-61	*"This thrust the burden of the action onto the Admiralty. under the leadership of the First Lord. Winston Churchill. and the First Sea Lord. Fleet Admiral Sir John (Jackie) Fisher. They envisioned a forcing of the straits by battleships which would bombard Istanbul and force Turkish capitulation."*
BODY-63	*"The Turks had been fortifying the straits for many years and a variety of forts, guns, and barriers were in place to prevent uninvited naval excursions."*
BODY-64	*"The attack was to occur in three parts, three bombardments at ever decreasing ranges, preceded by minesweepers which would clear the channel leading to the strait. The first day results were mixed. Ships of that day did not have continuous aiming fire control systems and the guns had to be relaid optically each time they were fired. They were therefore not especially accurate at long ranges and failed to completely reduce the forts."*
BODY-65	*"Cardens second in command. Vice Admiral De Robeck. led an attack right into the mouth of the straits. engaged the forts, and landed armed shore parties to capture the facilities and destroy the enemy guns."*
BODY-66	*"The crews of the minesweepers felt that it was simply too much. In the words on one of their officers. 'The men recognized sweeping risks and did not mind being blown up. but they hated the gunfire. and pointed out that they were not supposed to sweep under fire. they had not joined for that'."*
BODY-67	*"I do not understand why minesweepers should be interfered with by firing which causes no casualties. Two or three hundred casualties would be a moderate price to pay for sweeping up as far as the Narrows . . . This work has to be done whatever the loss of life and small craft and the sooner it is done the better."*
BODY-68	*"At 11:35 a.m. the assault began with Queen Elizabeth. Agamemmnon. Lord Nelson. and Inflexible engaging the forts at Chanak and Kilid Bahr which guarded the Narrows. The ships bombarded the forts until slightly after noon when the French battleships were called forward to carry out the close range attack on the inner defenses. This they did with vigor. and by 1:45 p.m. the Turkish fire had practically ceased."*
BODY-69	*"The British and French, believing that they had located all the minefields, were at a loss to explain the losses. One man gets the credit for this feat. Lieutenant Colonel Geehl, a Turkish coastal defense expert, had taken a small steamer, Nousret, into Eren Keui Bay on March 8th and laid a line of twenty mines."*
BODY-70	*"The Army must land and silence the guns before the fleet could open the straits and carry the attack to ~stanbul."*
BODY-71	*"The Allies now realized that the road to Istanbul could not be opened by action on the water alone. It was equally clear to me that they would not relinquish such a high prize without further effort . . . Hence, a large landing had to be counted upon."*
BODY-72	*"The peninsula was now for us little better than a bottomless pit: swallowing all the men and munitions we could throw into it. The Navy was left helpless off the beach with no more useful duty than to supply the needs of the Army, and protect it as far as the restricted use of its gun power permitted."*
BODY-73	*"The failure was due to several factors. First among these was technology. The mines in use by the Turks were moored contact mines of a type developed by the Russians in 1908 which were set to float at a predetermined depth. This depth is arrived at by*

computing the range of the tide, the average draft of your targets, and setting the length of the mooring cable to cover this range."

BODY-74 "The final, and most significant failure, was the failure of nerve on the part of the senior commander. Vice Admiral John De Robeck. By the time the Army landed, the minesweeping flotilla was larger, better trained, and better equipped than at any point previous. Nonetheless, he forswore the attempt despite the urgings of his chief of staff and the long-distance chiding of Churchill. The events of March 18th had demonstrated that the Turkish guns at the Narrows could be silenced by naval gunfire, and that being the case, the mines could be swept and the passage to Istanbul opened. This failure, more than any other, accounts for the tragedy of Gallipoli."

BODY-75 "In this case three ships were sunk and one seriously damaged attempting to force the fields."

BODY-76 "In this case all but four of thirty five minesweepers were lost or damaged while sweeping. The majority of these losses were to the overwatch fires and not to the mines themselves. This represents a casualty rate of 88.5%."

BODY-77 "At a sweep speed of five knots a channel through the entire Dardanelles could have been swept in eight hours."

BODY-78 "Over all things, war is the crucible of technology, and by the end of the war the belligerants had begun to develop the more sophisticated devices which would plague and please the sailors of World War II."

BODY-80 "The increasing liklihood of hostilities caused the U.S. Navy to contract for the 'Raven' class fleet minesweeper in 1938. The first of these 220 foot, steel hulled ships, USS Auk, was delivered on January 15, 1942."

BODY-81 "For reasons previously discussed in this thesis the major navies of the world hold mine warfare in poor regard and it tends to suffer from neglect between conflicts. In the 1920's and early 1930's the entire U.S. Navy's effort in the field consisted of one physicist attached to the Naval Ordnance Laboratory, designing mines which were never produced."

BODY-82 "The story of mine warfare at the Normandy invasion is largely a Royal Navy one. To understand the speed and efficiency with which they swept the invasion areas it is important to understand the depth of experience gained and level of effort they sustained between September 1939 and June 1944. The German efforts and the British parrys continued without letup for the entire war. Both parties developed new weapons and countermeasures constantly, and much of the development in this branch of naval warfare comes from this conflict."

BODY-83 "After determining the characteristics of the sensor mechanism the British were able to develop a countermeasure which they fielded in January 1940. This countermeasure initially took the form of a large magnetic coil mounted on a wooden barge and towed by a tugboat. It was followed by the first incidence of airborne mine countermeasures. Wellington bombers were fitted with magnetic coils and flown down channels at wavetop height. Both methods produced results but were not deemed the final answer."

BODY-84 "After some experimentation with various magnetic field generators in trawlers the LL sweep was developed. This swaoping tochniquo involvod tho towing o f two cables astern of the minesweeper which were electrically pulsed. This established a magnetic field which detonated the mine. This basic technique is still in use t0day."

BODY-85 "The accoustic mine was simply the latest in the technological war between to scientifically inclined enemies. These mines incorporated a simple microphone to capture the vibration made by a passing ships internal machinery. The initial model.

BODY-85 *first employed in October 1940. was uncomplicated and coarsely set. The coarser the mine setting. the more subject it is to actuation by any sound. rather than one specific to a particular type of ship. and the easier it is to sweep."*

BODY-86 *"By the end of 1941 the British Commonwealth Navies had amassed considerable experience in mine warfare. They had swept a total of 1407 magnetic mines. 992 acoustic mines. and 1042 contact mines. In the process they had lost 97 mine warfare ships of various types. as well as 11 larger warships and 291 merchants. 140 ships of various types had been damaged."*

BODY-87 *"An extensive exchange of liaison personnel began, with the USN observing and adopting the various British countermeasures techniques and equipment as they were adapted. One of the liaison officers, Ensign Charles Howard, became the USN's first mine warfare casualty when he was killed attempting to defuse a German magnetic mine."*

BODY-90 *"Assault sweeping technique was maturing rapidly by this point. The typical sequence of events would involve an initial fast clearance of the boat lanes by large minesweepers utilizing Oropesa sweeps. They would be lead by smaller launches conducting a 'skim sweep' with light rope sweep gear designed to remove moored mines close to the surface. An influence sweep using LL and SA gear would follow, usually conducted by the shallow draft YMS who would sweep to the minimum depth possible. They would be followed by small boats towing very light sweep gear to clear the very shallow water. Divers would clear inshore of these."*

BODY-91 *"The Germans had been fortifying the coast of France for some time. General Erwin Rommel, in command of German forces in France had developed a sophisticated and formidable obstacle system to prevent an amphibious assault. Prominant in his calculations was the integration of the sea mine into his obstacle system. Rommel was astute in his choice of a naval advisor. selecting Admiral Freidrich Ruge. an expert in coastal defense and a devotee of mine warfare."*

BODY-92 *"In the very shallow areas directly offshore they developed a new type of coastal mine. This device, known as coastal mine A resembled a giant Kewpie doll. The warhead was the weight on the bottom holding the mine upright, extending two meters upward from this was a two meter steel frame topped with a chemical horn contact fuze. When a sweeper struck this mine it merely rolled over, righting itself when the sweep gear was clear."*

BODY-94 *"This operation had to be carried out without alerting the Germans, as minesweeping would be seen as a definite indicator of impending assault. This was accomplished by..."*

BODY-95 *"The surprise of the assault was nearly lost when the minesweepers approached within eleven miles of the French coast on the day prior to the invasion. Admiral Ruge believes these units were observed but not reported. Had they been, and had the Germans reacted, they could hardly have failed to notice the massive concentration of shipping then building in Area Z and the adjacent channels."*

BODY-96 *"The assault began at 0630. 6 June 1944, taking the Germans by surprise. Among the many reasons why the Germans were surprised, a large portion of the credit must be given to the minesweeping force. Sufficient numbers were assembled to allow the rapid sweeping of a large area to an acceptable confidence level. The minesweeping forces had the advantage of, in the British case, nearly five years of experience dealing with the threat and had become masters in the field."*

BODY-97 *"The surprise prevented the Germans from using one of their newest undersea weapons. the pressure mine. from disrupting the invasion."*

BODY-98   "As mentioned in the preface to this chapter, amphibious assaults are notoriously sensitive to disruptions of timing and synchronization. The effect of such an unplanned speed restriction would be to disrupt buildup of the beachhead, deny fire support, and delay the movement of logistics over the shore. Because of the initial surprise, the Germans were unable to employ these weapons until the initial assault phases were ended, and the disruption, while significant, was not critical."

BODY-99   "In this case 48 ships were lost for a total of 1354 mines swept, yielding a loss ratio of 1 ship per 28.2 mines cleared. Total losses were less than one percent of the invasion force."

BODY-100 "The two MEB amphibious task force employed in Operation Desert Storm employed 31 ships. At the Normandy loss rate of one ship per 28.2 mines the force would have been eliminated."

BODY-101 "First, there is no substitute for numbers. The 85 minesweepers used at Utah were needed to open that beach quickly. Even with the massive air and naval bombardment it was impossible to completely isolate the beachhead and every additional hour worked in the Germans favor."

BODY-102 "The United States Pacific Fleet lost 99 percent of its over 500 mine warfare ships, 3000 officers, and 30,000 enlisted men."

BODY-103 "The Soviets had conducted extensive mining operations in World War II in the Baltic and Black Seas, and as mentioned in the introduction, had used mines early in the twentieth century against the Japanese at Port Authur. They had amassed large stockpiles of mines, and as an added bonus, had captured the German scientists and factories which were producing the advanced influence fuzed ground mines referred to in the Normandy study. They were in a unique position to assist the North Koreans in combatting a sea power."

BODY-104 "The Soviets conducted an analysis of the Korean coastline with an eye towards the most efficient use of m i n a n. Thay cnrrnatly aantnd that the wast. or Y ~ l l n w Sea Coast. is a mass of inlets. mudflats. and estuaries with a large tidal variation. It was thus not amenable to mining or amphibious operations. The east coast, bordered by the Sea of Japan, is the exact opposite. Due to the high eastern mountains most rivers in Korea drain to the west and the alluvial shallows found there are not present on the opposite shore. The coastline is straight, the water deep relatively close inshore, the currents and tidal range are small. It

BODY-105 "The tremendous success of the Inchon landing and its associated operations caused the collapse of North Korean organized resistance. The assault forces linked up with Allied forces advancing northward, recaptured Seoul, and began a northward pursuit of the rapidly withdrawing North Korean Peoples Army."

BODY-106 "Wonsan lies on the east coast of the Korean peninsula 80 miles north of the 38th parallel. It is in a large bay providing an excellent fleet anchorage with depths ranging from 10 fathoms to 15 feet over a hard sand bottom. Tides and currents are negligible. The beaches are of moderate gradient and good trafficability. There are good mobility corridors extending north, southwest, and west. In short, it is an obviously excellent choice for an amphibious objective area."

BODY-107 "The strong probability exists that the ports and possible landing beaches under control of the North Koreans have been recently mined. The sighting of new mines floating in the area indicates that mines are being seeded along the coast."

BODY-108 "The decision was made to land the X Corps at Wonsan, in an administrative vice tactical operation."

BODY-109 "The minefield had been laid by Koreans under the supervision of professional Soviet mine experts. Intelligence had reported the presence of thirty such Soviet personnel in the Wonsan area between 16 July and 4 October. They had designed a field which provided the optimum defensive barrier and was interlocked with overwatching shore batteries. Unbeknownst to the Americans, they had also planted delayed action magnetic mines in the field."

BODY-111 "The failure at Wonsan was tempered by the success of the ground forces so the actual tactical loss was insignificant. Nevertheless. it severly shocked a Navy which had grown accustomed to exercising complete control of the sea. The simple fact was that over 40,000 men were delayed offshore for five days, an event which could have proven fatal in differing circumstances. A similar occurance at Normandy would have been disasterous. It galvanized the Navy into building a fleet of over 150 non-magnetic minesweepers in the 1950's."

BODY-112 "In thin caaa. nn. Tho loss nf surprise, while complete, was negated by the rapid advance of the Eighth Army and their securing of the landing force's objectives."

BODY-113 "In this case no. No measure of the experienced versus the expected losses yield a potential loss of more than 12 %. In an eighteen ship MEB amphibious task force this would equate to a loss of two ships. The delay at Wonsan was more telling than the actual or potential losses."

BODY-114 "A new innovation was the use of helicopters and patrol aircraft to locate minefields. The coordination of these with the underwater demolition teams and surface minesweepers directly contributed to the low casualty rate."

BODY-115 "The real lesson of Wonsan was that the mine had not lost its usefulness, despite the primacy of the aircraft carrier and the jet aircraft in naval warfare. The Navy learned from this incident that the powerful amphibious forces are completely ineffective if they can't get ashore."

BODY-116 "Lacking resources, removed from the mainstream, and rarely operational, the minesweepers languished at Charleston, S.C., and Tacoma, WA. The force did not receive top flight personnel as the main stream navy focused elsewhere. The minesweeper became regarded chiefly as an early command opportunity, one to be completed and then left as rapidly as possible."

BODY-117 "The Germans pioneered the Troika system of remote control minesweeping craft, and the Italian shipbuilding industry perfected the use of glass reinforced plastic (GRP) as a substitute for wood."

BODY-119 "The war escalated in mid 1984 with the advent of what became known as the 'Tanker War'. This featured aircraft from both sides attacking merchant shipping bound for each others ports. The Iranians rapidly added a new twist as their navy began attacking shipping throughout the Persian Gulf."

BODY-121 "The exercise had a profound effect on the Iraqis. Several weeks after the conclusion of Imminent Thunder, the first floating mines began to appear in the vicinity of the Saudi oil field of Saffiniyeh. These mines were free of sea growth, indicating they had been recently laid, and of a design never before encountered. They were designated LUGM-145, after the Arabic acronym for mine, the 145 was the weight of the explosive charge in kilograms. The heavy weather had caused the Iraqi mines to part their moorings and float south on the prevailing current."

BODY-123 "The Tripoli struck a moored contact mine of the LUGM-145 variety. This mine opened a 16 by 20 foot hole in the hull, flooded three compartments, and caused the ship to temporarily lose power."

BODY-124 "The minesweepers found themselves on the fringes of two large minefields which blocked access to the Kuwaiti coastline. They began sweeping mines in earnest and by 25 February had cleared a 1000 yard channel through these mines to allow the battleships access to their firing positions."

BODY-125 "The magnetic disturbance of a large ship extends well beyond that distance and the larger amphibious assault ships are only exceeded in size by aircraft carriers. By pulsing the magnetic sweeping equipment at very high amperages, the minesweepers can detonate the mines outside the danger radius. Despite this assurance it is still a tedious and dangerous process."

BODY-126 "The truly discouraging feature of the Desert Storm mine warfare episode is our failure to heed the lessons we had just learned in Earnest Will. We knew that the Persian Gulf was particularly amenable to mining, and we knew the Iraqis had accumulated experience in mine warfare over their ten-year conflict with the Iranians. Nevertheless, we stumbled blindly into their minefields just as we had 41 years previously at Wonsan. The magnitude of this particular failure was eclipsed by the magnificence of the victory."

BODY-127 "Given the seven ships available the figure quoted was two to three weeks. The relationship is linear, so given 14 ships of similar capability, the time would be one to one and one half. To achieve clearance in twenty four hours 56 minesweepers would have been required, exactly twice the total in the entire Navy inventory in 1991."

BODY-128 "In this case yes. The postulated 3000-5000 man or 6-10 ship loss would have been sufficient to stop the assault or radically alter its nature."

BODY-129 "After some initial consternation, mine warfare is once again slipping towards oblivion."

BODY-131 "In the case of Normandy the answer is no. The mines employed there were absolutely state of the art and included some types never before encountered. While inflicting damage they did not delay the assault. and their effect, while substantial. was not critical."

BODY-132 "In the cases of Gallipoli and Normandy the answer is yes. In the case of Wonsan and Desert Storm surprise was not a factor."

BODY-133 "The answer depends on the level of threat and the degree of clearance confidence desired by the commander. As shown, to sweep a two MEB amphibious operating area in 24 hours to a confidence of 70% against a sophisticated threat requires 56 minesweepers. Wonsan was swept in 15 days by 35 minesweepers to a similar high level of confidence. Normandy was swept in 24 hours by over 300 ships, albeit to a lower level of confidence as shown by the higher loss rate."

BODY-134 "In all four cases there was no problem with basic technique. The problems, where they appeared, were due to levels of training and availability of forces."

BODY-135 "The failure at Gallipoli lengthened the battle on the western front and hastened the downfall of the Russian government. A failure at Normandy would have had incalculable consequences."

BODY-136 "I would recommend that further study be undertaken to design a mine countermeasures force capable of clearing a two MEB sized amphibious operating area to a high degree of confidence in 24 hours or less. Concurrent studies should be conducted to evaluate standards of readiness and training within the mine force, with an eye towards designing a system which would ensure these ships were always fully deployable and employable."

THE EFFECTS OF SEA MINING UPON AMPHIBIOUS WARFARE

A thesis presented to the Faculty of the U.S. Army
Command and General Staff College in partial
fullfillment of the requirements for the
degree

MASTER OF MILITARY ART AND SCIENCE

by

JAMES F. BALL, LCDR, USN
B.A., University of Hawaii, Honolulu, Hawaii, 1977

Fort Leavenworth, Kansas
1992

Approved for public release. Distribution is unlimited.

MASTER OF MILITARY ART AND SCIENCE
THESIS APPROVAL PAGE

Name of candidate: LCDR James F. Ball, USN

Title of thesis: The Effects of Sea Mining upon Amphibious Warfare.

Approved by:

_____, Thesis Committee Chairman
LTC Richard I. Kendall, M.S.

_____, Member
MAJ William B. Huben, M.A.

_____, Member, Consulting Faculty
LTC Earnest M. Pitt, J.D.

Accepted this 5th day of June 1992 by:

_____, Director, Graduate Degree Programs
Philip J. Brookes, Ph.D.

The opinions and conclusions expressed herein are those of the student author and do not necessarily represent the views of the U.S. Army Command and General Staff College or any government agency. (References to this study should contain the foregoing statement.)

ABSTRACT

THE EFFECTS OF SEA MINING UPON AMPHIBIOUS WARFARE by LCDR James F. Ball, USN, 138 pages

This study investigates the effects of sea mining upon amphibious warfare. The methodology involves case studies of amphibious assaults conducted at Gallipoli, Normandy, Wonsan, and the Persian Gulf during Operation Desert Storm. The cases are examined in terms of forces involved, mining conducted, and the effect the mining and the mine countermeasures had upon the achievement of surprise in the assault.

The study attempts to determine if the determining factor is the level of mine technology, the level of countermeasures technology, or the size of the forces committed. It emphasizes the importance of rapid and complete mine countermeasures to the achievement of surprise in the amphibious assault.

Based upon the four case studies conducted the determinant appears to be force levels. At Normandy, where levels were adequate, the operation was successful. At Gallipoli and Wonsan the results were either failure or inconclusive. The Persian Gulf study points out that failure would have been the likely result. A recommendation to prevent further deterioration of the mine countermeasures force is presented.

ACKNOWLEDGEMENTS

The assistance of Lieutenants Colonel Kendall and Pitt, and Major Huben, is gratefully acknowledged. Commander James Clark and Lieutenant Commander Homer Kaufman, both experts in the mine warfare field, contributed expert advice and support during the duration of this effort. The staff of the Combined Arms Research Library, through their efforts, made much of this work possible.

TABLE OF CONTENTS

	PAGE
ABSTRACT	iii
ACKNOWLEDGEMENTS	iv
LIST OF FIGURES	vi

CHAPTER

I. INTRODUCTION	1
Thesis Question	8
Definition of Terms	10
Historical Significance	14
II. REVIEW OF LITERATURE	33
Books	33
Periodicals	36
Government Publications	41
III. METHODS AND PROCEDURES	43
IV. CASE STUDIES IN MINE WARFARE	45
Introduction	45
Gallipoli Study	49
Normandy Study	72
Wonsan Study	96
Desert Storm Study	110
V. CONCLUSIONS AND RECOMMENDATIONS	125
APPENDIX	131
BIBLIOGRAPHY	135

LIST OF FIGURES

FIGURE		PAGE
1.	Relative Costs of WWII Mining and Submarine Campaigns	5
2.	Russo-Japanese War Mining Losses	15
3.	World War I Mining Losses	17
4.	German Influence Mines	19
5.	Minesweeper Losses in World War II	24
6.	Mines Laid and Swept in World War II	25
7.	Gallipoli Shore Batteries	56
8.	Gallipoli Assault Formation	58
9.	Mine Caused Speed Restrictions at Normandy	92
10.	Minesweepers in Commission 1946-1953	96

CHAPTER ONE

INTRODUCTION

The ability of the U.S. Navy to conduct timely mine clearance operations has fallen to a dangerously low level. Large magnitude sweep operations such as those required to rapidly clear the areas needed for large scale amphibious operations are no longer possible. Effective levels of mine clearance will require long periods of time, telegraph the intent to conduct an amphibious assault, and make such an operation tactically unfeasible.

Of all the forms of naval warfare, mining is arguably the most cost effective. A well conceived and properly laid minefield presents a constant and serious threat to enemy vessels and is minimally affected by weather or environmental conditions. It may be planned to suit a variety of operational scenarios. It may be defensive, designed to protect friendly ports or coastal areas, or it may be offensive, designed to attack the enemy in his harbors and deny him the use of the sea.

Mining may be covert or overt, either approach still requires the direction of valuable and scarce resources to mine countermeasures. It also requires an investment of time, the scarcest and most fragile of resources in military operations. To achieve this effect it is not necessary to lay a single mine, the mere announcement of mining still requires that an opponent commit resources for verification.

Mines do not grow obsolete. The moored contact mine has been in the arsenal since the American Civil War. The chemical horn fused spherical moored mined laid by the Iranians in 1986-88 and by the Iraqi's in 1990-91 are copies of a Russian design dating from 1908. Ground influence mines that use magnetic, acoustic, or pressure fusing were developed by the Germans and operationally employed during World War II. Since that time, there has been considerable improvement in these devices but no change in the basic operating concept.

However, there has been a quantum leap in the sophistication of the mine, and a number of mine manufacturers are offering to upgrade older mines with modern electronics and sensors.[1] A typical sophisticated anti-landing mine is the Manta, made by Misar S.p.A. of Brescia ,Italy. This is a 200 Kilogram mine, trapezoidal in shape, with a glass-reinforced plastic (GRP) outer case. It functions in a depth range from 2.5 to 100 meters and has an effective range of 20-30 meters. The Manta features dual fusing, it is acoustically armed and fired by magnetic signature. A hydrostatic anti-handling device will detonate the mine if it is lifted from the bottom. The weapon can be

---

[1] Klaus Benz, "Mine Warfare at Sea", Armada International, 14 (Dec/Jan 1990-91): 28-34

set to arm at any time up to 63 days after laying, has a 511 day operational life in the water, and has a storage life of 30 years.[2] A Manta is believed responsible for the damage sustained by the USS Princeton (CG-59) in the Persian Gulf on 18 February 1991. The Bofors GMI 100 Rockan offers comparable features, with an added advantage. The mine has a waterplane shape that allows it to be laid directly from a seawall. The shape is engineered so that the mine glides horizontally to a distance twice the water depth.[3]

There has not been a corresponding quantum leap in mine countermeasures technology. With some changes, mines are still cleared much the same way they were cleared during World War II. Moored contact mines are positively buoyant; i.e., they float, and are swept by cutting them free of their moorings. This is accomplished by towing a long wire behind a minesweeper which veers down to a preset depth and out to a preset distance. Cutting devices are attached to this wire and as the mine anchor cables slide down the sweep wire they are captured and severed. The mines then float to the surface and are disposed of in a variety of fashions.

Influence mines are more difficult to clear. Magnetically fuzed mines are swept by pulsing a large

---

[2] " Italy's Mine Makers", *International Defense Review*, 15 (Mar 1983): 369.

[3] Mark Hewish, "Protecting Coastal Waters", *International Defense Review*, 20 (Jan 1988): 29-32.

electrical current into the water from a cable towed by a minesweeper. Acoustically fuzed mined can be detonated by introducing noise into the water. The magnetic field generated by a ship can be reduced by the processes of deperming or degaussing. The magnetic sweeping, acoustic sweeping, and magnetic field reduction techniques were developed by the British during World War II in response to German mining operations.[4]

Modern influence mines require clearance techniques which are a sophisticated version of those mentioned above. Mines like the above mentioned Manta can be equipped with a variety of devices to counter sweep attempts. Ship counters, which can be set so a mine ignores a certain number of ships before detonating, are quite common. Variable arming delays are available which turn mines on and off at predetermined times. Mines no longer conform to the classic cylindrical or spherical shapes so their detection with sonar is much more difficult. Non-ferrous material is now commonly used for mine cases and moorings with a corresponding reduction in the magnetic signature of the mine. Valsella S.p.A., an Italian mine maker, offers the VS-SS5, a small mine laid in clusters around larger mines, which will detect and destroy approaching minesweeping

---

[4] Peter Elliot, *Allied Minesweeping in World War II.* (Annapolis, Naval Institute Press, 1979) 34.

equipment.[5] Finally, integrated circuit technology has allowed the development of small memory devices for mines which allow the mines to be programmed for specific targets while ignoring others.

Costs of Mining/Submarine Campaigns

	MINING	SUBMARINES
Enemy casualties in tons/month	280,000	110,000
US ship investment per enemy ton casualty	$16	$100
Tons of enemy casualties per crewman required	3500	560
Tons of enemy casualty per crewman lost	12,000	1200
Costs of US losses per enemy ton casualty	$6.00	$55.00

FIGURE ONE

---

[5] " Naval Mine Warfare", *International Defense Review Editorial Supplement*, (Nov 1986).

Mines are proliferating. The sea mine is viewed as a purely defensive weapon by the majority of the world. As such, there are little restrictions on their sale and mines are generally made available to any country which can afford them. Both the United States and the Soviet Union have exported large numbers as part of their military aid programmes. Italy, in particular, has developed a sophisticated mine manufacturing industry that aggressively pursues sales abroad. Misar, Valsella, and Technovar make a complete spectrum of mines for almost every imaginable application, including a number which are purpose-built for countering amphibious landings.

Other firms, such as Bofors A.G. of Sweden and British Aerospace and Electronics (BAE) also aggressively market sophisticated mines. For those who cannot afford the low cost of new mines, these companies offer packages which upgrade their existing arsenals to modern specifications.[6]

Basic mines are not difficult to manufacture for a country with an established weapons industry. The Iranians made and employed hundreds of mines known as SADAF-02, copies of the Russian M-08 design dating almost to the turn of the century. The Iraqis undertook a similar effort during Desert Storm, and prior to the war exhibited and

---

[6] Benz, 28. The Chinese firm of Dalien, BAE of the United Kingdom, and Misar of Italy all offer such programmes.

offered for sale a variety of mines, some quite sophisticated.

Mines are arguably the most cost effective weapon available in the world. An Iranian SADAF-02 caused over $150 million in damage to the USS Samuel B. Roberts in 1988. Two Iraqi mines caused over $40 million in damage to USS Tripoli and USS Princeton. A naval officer offered the following comment,

> "They are cheap, reasonably simple, reliable, producible in great numbers, easily stockpiled, and possess a devastating wallop. They require countermeasures which demand a great investment in forces and technology. For those who wage naval war, these are virtues to esteem. In pounds of explosive per dollar they are naval warfare's greatest bargain".[7]

The Naval Ordnance Laboratory conducted an analysis after World War II to determine which of the campaigns against Japanese shipping, the mining or the submarine, was most cost effective. The results are illuminating and are depicted in Figure 1.

Finally, mines are absurdly easy to employ. The United States and other technologically advanced nations use sophisticated mine laying techniques utilizing a variety of platforms. This allows the minefields to be emplaced with speed and precision. However, if neither is required, then any surface vessel can be used as a minelayer, the Iranians

---

[7] Robert H. Smith, *United States Naval Institute Proceedings*, 106 (Apr 1980): 29.

used landing craft, the Iraqis used a tug, and the Koreans and Vietnamese used sampans, all effectively.

From the introduction it is possible to see that mines are a significant threat to naval operations in all areas. Chief among the U.S. Navy's many missions is power projection, of which amphibious warfare plays an inportant part. It is essential to almost all types of forced entry operations, and plays a paramount role throughout the operational continuum. Because of the inherently fragile nature of amphibious assaults success often depends upon surprise. The increasing sophistication of mines, their proliferation, and the decrease in mine countermeasure forces may have rendered such surprise unattainable. Therefore, the primary research question of this thesis shall be: <u>Has the proliferation of high technology sea mines eliminated tactical surprise in large-scale amphibious assaults?</u>

Subordinate Questions:

    a. Does the loss of tactical surprise make a large-scale amphibious operation unfeasible?

    b. Based on historical data, what level of losses can be expected by amphibious forces entering a mined area?

    c. What level of mine clearance effort is required to sweep an amphibious operating area for a large-scale assault?

d. Given c. above, and assets available in 1991, what would be the duration of such a sweep effort?

e. Would the sweep effort alert an enemy to potential landing areas?

f. Given historical data, what level of losses can be expected by the mine clearance forces?

g. Given b. and f. above, and current force levels would expected losses render an amphibious assault force combat ineffective?

h. Are current minesweeping techniques adequate to clear an amphibious operating area in a timely manner?

i. How does mine technology affect the duration of mine sweeping operations?

j. Is the potential loss of the large scale amphibious option a matter of great concern in the current strategic environment?

The following assumptions are incorporated into the research and conclusions of this thesis:

1. That mine technology will continue to improve.

2. That mines will continue to be freely sold on world weapons markets.

3. That there will be no change in current and projected U.S. Navy force structure.

4. That amphibious assault will continue to be regarded as a desirable means of power projection.

5. That the likelihood of achieving surprise in an amphibious assault is inversely proportional to the amount of time devoted to mine clearance

Amphibious and mine warfare writings are heavily laced with jargon and technical terminology. To aid in understanding and provide clarification the following definition of terms is provided:

1. Amphibious operation: An attack launched from the sea by naval and landing forces, embarked in ships or craft involving a landing on a hostile shore. As an entity, an amphibious operation consists of five phases, planning embarkation, rehearsal, movement, and assault. Amphibious operations are divided into assaults, raids, demonstrations, and withdrawals.

2. Amphibious assault: The principal type of amphibious operation which involves establishing a force on a hostile shore.

3. Amphibious Objective Area: A geographical area, delineated in the initiating directive, for purposes of command and control within which is located the objective to be secured by the amphibious task force. This area must be of sufficient size to ensure accomplishment of the amphibious task force's mission and must provide sufficient area for conducting necessary sea, air, and land operations.

4. Amphibious lift: The total capacity of assault shipping utilized in an amphibious operation.

expressed in terms of personnel, vehicles, and measurement or weight tons of supplies.

5. Sea Echelon: A portion of the assault shipping which withdraws from or remains out of the transport area during an amphibious landing and operates in designated areas to seaward in an on-call or unscheduled status.

6. Transport area: An area assigned for the purpose of debarking troops and equipment.

7. Fire Support Area: An appropriate maneuver area assigned to fire support ships from which to deliver gunfire support to an amphibious operation.

8. Line of departure: A suitable marked offshore coordinating line to assist assault craft to land on designated beaches at scheduled times.

9. Boat Lane: A lane for amphibious assault landing craft, which extends seawards from the landing beaches to the line of departure. The width of the lanes is determined by the width of the corresponding beach.

10. Assault echelon: The element of a force that is scheduled for initial assault on the objective area.

11. Assault follow on echelons: That echelon of the assault troops, vehicles, aircraft equipment, and supplies which, while not needed to initiate the assault, is required to support and sustain the assault.

12. Commander, Amphibious Task Force: The commander of the naval and ground forces involved in an amphibious operation. Command of the landing force is relinquished when the Commander, Landing Force has established his headquarters ashore.

13. Commander, Landing Force: The commander of the assault elements of an amphibious operation.

14. Landing Area: That part of the objective area within which are conducted the landing operations of an amphibious force. It includes the beach, the approaches to the beach, the transport areas, the fire support areas, the air occupied by close supporting aircraft, and the land included in the advance inland to the initial objective.

15. Landing Site: A continuous segment of coastline over which troops, equipment, and supplies can be landed by surface means.

16. Landing Beach: That portion of a coastline usually required for the landing of a battalion landing team. Also identified as a tactical locality over which a force larger or smaller than a battalion may be landed.

17. Landing Craft: A craft employed in amphibious operations, specifically designed for carrying troops and equipment and for beaching, unloading, and retracting.

18. Landing force: A task organization of troops assigned to an amphibious assault.

19. Mine: An explosive device laid in the water with the intention of damaging or sinking ships or of deterring shipping from entering an area.

20. Mineable water: Waters where naval mines of any given type may be effective against any given target.

21. Mined area: An area declared dangerous due to the presence or suspected presence of mines.

22. Minefield: An area of water containing mines laid with or without a pattern.

23. Mine hunting: The employment of ships, aircraft, or divers to locate and dispose of individual mines.

24. Mine sweeping: The technique of searching for or clearing mines using mechanical or explosive gear, which removes or destroys the mine, or produces, in the area, the influence fields necessary to actuate it.

25. Influence Mine: A mine actuated by the effect of a target on some physical condition in the vicinity of the mine or on radiations emanating from the mine. Common types are magnetic, acoustic, pressure, and seismic.

26. Contact mine: A mine actuated by physical contact with a target.

27. Moored mine: A mine of positive buoyancy held below the surface by a mooring attached to a sinker or anchor on the bottom.

28. Bottom mine: A mine of negative buoyancy which remains on the seabed. Also known as a ground mine.

29. Beach minefield: A mine field laid in the very shallow water approaches to a beach, typically inside the three and one-half fathom (21 feet) depth curve.

Data presented in support of this thesis shall have the following limitations:

1. Data from 1914 to present.
2. Mine effects on amphibious operations.
3. United States and NATO mine clearance capabilities.
4. Western European and USSR mine technology.
5. Unclassified open-source data.

This study shall be significant in that it will serve to draw attention to the potential loss of a powerful tool of power projection, the amphibious assault. The Navy must once again be made aware of the unique vulnerability of large scale surface amphibious assaults to mine warfare and must make every effort to ensure that mine countermeasures capability does not deteriorate past the point that a rapid assault through a mined area is no longer possible. A secondary significance will be to open debate on counter-amphibious mining as a unique subset of mine warfare.

Mines have long been used as an instrument of naval warfare. The explosive kegs Bushnell floated down the

Delaware and the torpedoes which Farragut damned as he entered Mobile Bay were in fact mines. During the course of the Civil War the Union Navy suffered considerable loss from these devices, particularly in the restricted waters of the Mississippi River. Twenty seven Union ships were lost to mines during the Civil War while only nine were lost to shore batteries.[8]

During the Russo-Japanese War both sides employed mines liberally. The Russians used mines extensively during the siege of Port Arthur, specifically to deter a landing by the Japanese Army. The Japanese lost eleven ships, including two battleships, to Russian mines and were forced to take the base by siege from landward. Figure Two shows losses to mines during the Russo-Japanese War.[9]

Type	Russian	Japanese	Total
Battleship	1	2	3
Cruiser	1*	1	2
Coaster	0	2	2
Minelayer	1*	0	1
Destroyer	1	2	3
Gunboat	2	2	4
Totals	6	9	15

Figure Two
* Sunk by friendly mines

---

[8] U.S. Army Command and General Staff College. *Student Text 100-1 Navy and Marine Corps*, Ft. Leavenworth, KS: Department of the Army. 8-17

[9] Oliver W. Bagby, "Naval Mining and Naval Mines", *United States Naval Institute Proceedings*, 51 (DEC 1925) 2244-2257.

Mines had their first major effect during World War I. When the Gallipoli operation commenced, Allied naval forces attempting to force the Dardanelles and bombard Istanbul were met by dense Turkish minefields. These minefields accomplished two missions, they directly sank a number of ships, and they forced the ships into defined areas which were covered by coastal artillery. The Allies were forced to retreat and the decision was made to take Istanbul by amphibious assault via the Gallipoli peninsula. The Turks employed controlled mines in connection with other obstacles to canalize the allied landing efforts.[10] The minefields restricted the area available for fire support, assault, and resupply shipping. They also prevented Allied naval forces from interdicting the lines of communication extending from Istanbul to the Gallipoli Peninsula, allowing Axis forces unrestricted resupply and reinforcement. Allied forces were eventually forced to withdraw and the magnitude of the defeat was nearly the death knell for amphibious warfare.

World War I also provides the example of the North Sea Barrage. Allied forces, attempting to restrict German access to the Atlantic Ocean, placed over 60,000 mines in an enormous barrier across the North Sea extending from the Orkneys to Norway. These mines were partially effective in reducing the German U-Boat menace, accounting

---

[10] Ibid. 2249

for six submarines, but were at least an equal headache to the Allies in that they had to clear them at wars end, losing several ships in the process.[11] Once laid mines recognize no flags.

Approximately 205,000 mines were laid in World War I, resulting in the loss of 63 Allied and 60 Central Powers warships. A detailed breakdown of losses is provided below.[12]

Type	Allied	Central	Total
Battleship	6	0	6
Cruiser	3	2	5
Light Cruiser	2	2	4
Torpedo gunboat	2	0	2
Monitor	1	2	3
Sloop	5	0	5
Destroyer	28	15	43
Torpedo Boat	6	10	16
Minecraft	1	23	24
Auxiliary	2	0	2
Others	3	0	3
Submarines	4	6	10
Totals	63	60	123

Figure Three

There were two great mining campaigns in World War II, one conducted by the Germans against the Allies, and one conducted by the Americans against the Japanese. The German campaign began at the onset of war in 1939. Extensive

---

[11] Ibid. 2248.

[12] Ibid. 2247.

mining was conducted in the English Channel, the North Sea, and the Norwegian fiords. Utilizing first motor torpedo boats and destroyers, and later aircraft, the Germans heavily mined British waters. On one occasion the Thames was closed for 36 hours while the channel was swept.[13]

      After Pearl Harbor the Germans initiated Operation Paukenschlag (Drumroll), an attack by submarine on coastal traffic off the U.S. Eastern Seaboard. U-Boats laid small minefields off the approaches to New York harbor and the Chesapeake Bay, forcing the brief closure of both. Wilmington, NC, and Charleston, SC were closed for eight and ten days respectively. The fields were effective, one thirty mine field laid at the Chesapeake approaches in June 1942 sank or damaged four ships before it was cleared.[14]

The Germans inaugurated the use of submarines and aircraft as mine layers, and introduced magnetic, acoustic, and pressure fuzing to the world of mine warfare. The first magnetic mines were operationally employed in the fall of 1939, rapidly followed by acoustic and pressure activated mines.[15] These mines were normally laid by aircraft with parachute retardation. Later when arming delays made it safer surface craft were used. Due to the crude sensors of

---

[13] Peter Elliot. *Allied Minesweeping in World War II*. (Annapolis, Naval Institute Press, 1979): 31.

[14] Ibid. 70.

[15] Ibid. 30.

the time the mines were found to be most effective in shallow water. While a contact mine would blow a large hole in a ships hull, a ground influence mine would normally break a ships back without rupturing the hull. This type of damage would take many months in a dockyard to repair, and at worst, would cause the ship to be written off as a total loss, a not uncommon occurrence.[16] The Germans primarily employed six types of influence mines:[17]

German Influence Mines

Designator	Fuzing	Comments
G	Magnetic	Coarse sensitivity. Long slow pulse required for activation. Ideal for slower targets
AM MK 1	Dual Mag/acoustic	
A2	Acoustic	Increased sensitivity. 12 ship counter installed. Easily swept.
MA 101	Dual Mag/acoustic	4 microphones in parallel. Used sound build up to detonate.
A 104	Acoustic	10 ship counter.
A 105	Acoustic	Explosive sweep required

Figure Four

---

[16] Ibid. 24.

[17] Ibid. 54.

They chose this as an effective and inexpensive way to combat the Royal Navy, the only British force not matched in size and quality by the Axis. During the Dunkirk evacuation, an amphibious withdrawal, the British lost 7 minesweepers. An additional five were damaged but made port.[18]

The British were caught at the beginning of the war with a tiny mine countermeasures force, and responded to the German effort with a wholesale construction program and by large conversions of commercial fishing boats to mine sweepers. Over 800 commercial vessels were requisitioned for minesweeping duties by the Royal Navy at the start of World War II. Of these 223 were sunk while sweeping German mines.[19] German technology forced the British to develop magnetic and acoustic minesweeping methods which are still in use today.

By June 1944, the Germans had constructed extensive defensive minefields along the French coast, particularly in those areas they deemed vulnerable to amphibious assault. Additionally, they had emplaced offensive fields in the departure channels of British ports and along likely courses leading from those ports to the invasion beaches. Noting that the Allies did not mine the Bay of the Seine, the

---

[18] Ibid. 35.

[19] Ibid. 30.

Germans correctly deduced that it was a likely invasion area and heavily mined it. Hitler commented,

> " We have got to lay mines and still more mines in the Seine Bay with the tenacity of a bulldog. It is incomparably more effective to sink a whole cargo at sea than to have to fight the unloaded material and personnel on land".[20]

To maintain surprise the fields could not be swept until immediately prior to the invasion. The allies had, by this time, amassed a large fleet of mine craft, over 2000 total, and were able to sweep the channels and beach approach lanes in slightly more than 24 hours. Surprise was nearly lost when minesweeping units approached within visual range of the French coast on 5 June 1944. The senior German naval officer at Normandy, Admiral Friedrich Ruge, believes the units were sighted but not reported. Such a report would have led to the discovery of the invasion fleet and allowed the Germans an additional 24 hours to prepare their defenses.[21] The success at Normandy was due in large part to this effort, made possible by the early recognition of a substantial threat and the early commitment of resources to combat it. Even with the mine clearance effort sixteen ships were lost to mines during the operation.

---

[20] Arnold Lott, *Most Dangerous Sea*, (Annapolis, Naval Institute Press, 1959). 189.

[21] Friedrich Ruge, *Rommel In Normandy*, (San Rafael, Presidio Press, 1979). 176

The Germans gave considerable thought to the defensive mine fields surrounding Normandy, designing complicated mixed-type fields covered by large caliber coastal artillery. Recognizing that fields in shallow water are particularly difficult to sweep they developed a series of shallow water mines designed to destroy landing craft. This concept did not reach fruition as the German Navy, in charge of the mining, disagreed with the Army and held back its efforts.[22]

Recognizing the utility of mine warfare, the United States employed substantial numbers of mines against the Japanese. The shallow waters around the Japanese home islands and the large numbers of restricted straits and choke points make Japan particularly vulnerable to this method of warfare. Using submarines initially, and later aircraft, the U.S. Navy and Army Air Corps conducted Operation Starvation, laying thousands of sophisticated mines around the Japanese home islands, causing great losses to their naval and merchant fleets.

The Japanese had no effective minesweeping capability, despite their earlier lessons from the Russians, and were powerless in the face of this campaign which struck directly

---

[22] Ibid. 175. The German Army and Navy were not noted for their cooperation. A specific mine type had been developed to counter the Allied landing craft threat but it's production and deployment were delayed by the local German Naval Headquarters. Admiral Ruge was assigned to Rommel's staff and had no authority over local naval commanders.

at the strategic sea lines of communication over which Japan was receiving the majority of her raw materials. This campaign sank or damaged one-fourth of the prewar strength of the Japanese merchant marine at a minor cost to the Allied Forces. The significance of this event was that for the first time in the history of warfare a powerful nation had been strategically blockaded by an enemy who was forced to risk only a small portion of his forces. Japanese leaders estimated that the mining campaign was equally as effective as the bombing campaign.[23]

Most of these weapons were policed up by American occupation forces after the war. American forces employed mines so profusely during the Second World War than we often had to sweep through our own mines to gain access to invasion beaches, suffering losses in the process both from enemy fire and friendly mines. During the course of the war 27 allied ships were lost in U.S. fields alone.[24] Well into the 1960's these mines were continuing to claim victims. The following figures serve to illustrate the magnitude of the task.[25]

---

[23] Colin Ostrander, "Chaos at Shimonoseki", United States Naval Institute Proceedings, 73 (June 1947): 655. Out of the 1528 Superfortresses involved, 15 were shot down. This loss rate of approximately one percent compares favorably with the main bombing campaign, where losses averaged two percent.

[24] Lott. 294.

[25] Lott. 288-295.

Minesweeper Losses in World War II

Large Sweepers	Atlantic	Med	Pacific	Total
Royal Navy	21	21	3	45
Royal Australian Navy	0	0	4	4
Royal Canadian Navy	4	0	0	4
United States Navy	2	4	20	26
Small Sweepers	261	63	29	353
Totals	288	88	56	432

Figure Five

Mines Laid and Swept in World War II

Laid				Swept		
	Moored	Ground	total	Moored	Ground	total
Lant	97,000	23,000	120,000	2569	5926	8495
Med	30,000	25,000	55,000	7460	663	8123
Pacific	30,000	21,000	51,000	6000	6000	12,000
Total	157,000	79,000	226,000	16,029	12,589	28,618

Figure Six

World War II served as the genesis of a number of technological advance in mine warfare. Already mentioned is the German development of the influence fuze in its various permutations, an innovation rapidly copied by the allies. The British developed and fielded a number of minesweeping devices, the first magnetic and acoustic sweeps, and by placing large magnetic coils in a Wellington bomber and flying at wavetop height they introduced the first airborne mine countermeasures.[26] An American Lieutenant Commander

---

[26] Elliot. 32.

named Hyman Rickover did important work in magnetic sweeping, the first of his many contributions, and the University of California at San Diego developed the first high frequency mine hunting sonar.[27]

After the great demobilization following World War II the U.S. Navy in general, and the mine forces in particular, had been greatly reduced in number and capability. This mission had been primarily conducted by the reserves, and with their departure from active service the ability both to employ and counter mines was attenuated.

At this point it is worthy to note the position that the mine warfare mission held in the naval hierarchy. This particular form of naval warfare has always been regarded as unglamorous. It is physically difficult, particularly dangerous, and does not offer the glamour and excitement of service in the cruiser or destroyer forces, the prestige of aviation, or the benefits of service in a submarine. Perhaps most critically, particularly in peacetime, it is a career swamp. Senior officers ordered to duty in the mine forces have had the kiss of death laid on their careers. One First Lord of the British Admiralty summarized the prevalent attitude with the following comment, "... unpleasant work for a naval officer, an occupation like rat catching".[28]

---

[27] Lott, 66.

[28] Ibid, 17-19.

The post World War II focus on nuclear weaponry and high performance aircraft combined with the drastic reduction in budgets caused the Navy to quickly cast off its mine warfare forces. The force available in 1950 was but a shadow of that afloat only five years previously, ninety-nine percent of which had been deactivated. The Korean War was to provide the Navy with another lesson, its third in the 20th century, on the importance of mine warfare. The North Koreans had no effective naval capability against the USN, which ranged freely along the Korean coast, projecting power inland via naval air and long-range gunnery. They discovered, with the help of their Soviet mentors, that the naval mine is a poor mans friend, a weapon whose effect is extremely disproportionate to its cost.

Following the successful amphibious operation at Inchon, where only one small enemy field was discovered, Gen. Macarthur decided to attempt a repeat performance at the North Korean port city of Wonsan on the east coast of the peninsula. The amphibious task force arrived only to find that the area had been heavily mined and that the beaches were unapproachable. Nearly one week and three minesweepers later, the Second Marine Division landed at Wonsan long after the ground forces had overrun the area and were far to the north. The task force commander lamented,

> We have lost control of the seas to a nation without a navy, using pre World War One weapons, laid by vessels which were utilized at the time of the birth of Christ.[29]

Admiral Forest Sherman, then Chief of Naval Operations said,

> They caught us with our pants down. Those damn mines cost us eight days delay in getting the troops ashore and more than two hundred casualties. That's bad enough, but I can all too easily think of circumstances when eight days delay offshore could mean losing a war...We've been plenty submarine conscious and air conscious. Now we're going to start getting mine conscious-beginning last week.[30]

Mines continued to plague United Nations operations throughout the remainder of the Korean War. The amphibious withdrawal of forces from Hungham following the Chinese intervention required a heavy minesweeping effort, one fortunately possible by that time. Logistics over the shore, naval gunfire, and port operations were all effected as the North Koreans continued to lay mines using small fishing junks. A major expansion of the mine warfare force allowed the UN forces to cope with this threat.[31]

---

[29] C. R. Wages, "Mines . . . The Weapons that Wait", United States Naval Institute Proceedings 88(May 1962): 103.

[30] Lott, 277.

[31] Paolo Coletta, United States Naval Institute Proceedings 85 (Nov 1959): 82. The best benefit of this debacle was that it provoked experimentation into novel countermeasures. Aircraft, helicopters, and combat swimmers were used to detect mines, and unsuccessful attempt at countermining with bombs was attempted, and a splinter fleet of motor launches

After the lessons of the Korean War the Navy greatly expanded the mine force and when Vietnam arrived they were ready for a challenge that failed to materialize. Some isolated incidents occurred, primarily in port areas, and largely as a result of direct actions by combat swimmers. Such operations, when encountered, were dealt with by naval special operations forces. The U.S. did use mines to close Haiphong harbor in 1972, and the only large scale mine clearance operation during the war was Operation End Sweep, our post-war removal of the weapons. This operation featured the first large scale use of the CH-53 helicopter to tow minesweeping equipment.

Following the Vietnam War the U.S. Navy began an extensive drawdown. Many of the ships had been run hard with little maintenance for years and were found to be beyond economical repair. The mine forces were sharply cut and what resources remained were dedicated to development of the airborne option. These forces were used in the multi-national clearance of the Suez Canal following the Camp David Accords, and to clear the harbor of Jeddah, Saudi Arabia after the Libyan mining in 1985. Both operations were limited in scope and executed in a benign environment.

---

was used for minesweeping. These launches were the genesis of the 57 foot MSB (minesweeping boat).

The advent of the Iran-Iraq war in 1980 found both antagonists well equipped with mines and willing to use them. The Persian Gulf is arguably one of the most mineable bodies of water in the world. It is shallow, not exceeding 200 feet of depth across most of its expanse and it is sharply compartmented by shallows, oil fields, and various other unnavigable areas. Little tactical or technical sophistication is needed to effectively mine anywhere in the Gulf. Both sides mined each others harbors and naval bases, and as the Arab countries began to actively support Iraq the Iranians began to covertly mine their harbors and oil production facilities.

The United States essentially entered the conflict in May 1987 when the USS Stark was damaged by an Iraqi Exocet missile while on patrol northeast of Jubail, Saudi Arabia. The increasing US involvement coupled with strengthening Arab support for Iraq caused the Iranians to respond, like the North Koreans, with the poor mans weapon. As more and more vessels began to strike mines in the Gulf the U.S. responded by deploying a mine countermeasures force, initially airborne only, followed by surface vessels. The force began operations in late 1987 and continued until early 1990, when they returned to the United States. Despite their efforts the Iranians continued to mine more or less at will until the war ended in the summer of 1988.

The mine countermeasures force returned to the Persian Gulf less than six months after returning home. Responding to the increased U.S. naval presence in the Gulf, and the threat of amphibious assault, Iraq began to heavily mine the northern reaches of the Persian Gulf in November 1990. Floating mines began to appear in the areas south of Kuwait by Thanksgiving 1990. The Iraqis continued to mine until their forces were destroyed. U.S., British, and Saudi minesweepers were able to sweep two long narrow channels to enable the use of battleship gunfire but were unable to clear sufficient area for the amphibious task force. Had an assault been required the amphibious task force would have been forced into incompletely swept water, placeing 31 ships and over 30,000 personnel at severe risk. Had adequate mine clearance forces been available the amphibious task force could have covered a much larger area and tied down more troops, and naval gunfire shipd could have provided more timely and accurate support to forces advancing north up the coast.[32] The USS Tripoli and the USS Princeton were both heavily damaged by Iraq mines during the operation.

The Iraqis admitted to emplaceing slightly over 1600 mines in the northern Persian Gulf. The US, British, Belgian, Australian, and Saudi minesweeping force completed clearing these mines in September 1991. Undoubtedly,

---

[32] Norman Friedman, "The Seaward Flank", United States Naval Institute Proceedings, 117 (Jul 1991): 81-83.

residual mines from these fields will plague mariners in the Persian Gulf for years to come.

The significance of this study is to determine if we have possibly once again allowed our mine countermeasures forces to deteriorate to dangerous levels, and by doing so lost or severely compromised our ability to conduct major amphibious assaults in a timely manner. Amphibious assaults depend heavily on surprise for a successful outcome and the activities of a mine sweeping force are difficult to conceal. Small numbers of minesweepers lengthen the clearance times and invite a possibly fatal compromise.

Chapter Two

Review of Literature

Literature on the subject of mine warfare is divided roughly into tactical and technical branches, further subdivided into books, professional journals and periodicals. There is also a limited amount of primary source material available locally, primarily in the form of fleet lessons learned and after action reports.

Literature on mine warfare is cyclic in nature and its volume corresponds to level of interest at the time. During the course of my initial research I examined the indices for Naval Institute Proceedings from 1900 to the present. A rash of articles appear in 1900, 1918-1920, 1945, 1950-1953, and 1988-1990. These writings reflect interest after the Russo-Japanese War, World Wars One and Two, Korea, and the Persian Gulf conflict. Similar patterns are exhibited to a lesser degree in military trade journals such as International Defense Review, Janes Defense Weekly, Seapower, and Armada International.

There are few books written on mining, and none focus exclusively on its amphibious aspects. Allied Minesweeping in World War Two is a detailed study of mine warfare in the European Theater of Operations in World War Two. The book provides an excellent overview of the major amphibious operations in the ETO, and the mine sweeping effort that was required to support each. Also provided are a series of tables detailing forces, losses, and mining efforts by the various powers. Published by the Naval Institute Press, it is a technical history above all else.

A Most Dangerous Sea is a similar, less detailed, and somewhat anecdotal history that is oriented more towards the American contribution to mine warfare. This history also covers the Korean war. It supplements the mass of detail presented in Allied Minesweeping in World War II and provides insight into the organization and service politics of the American mine force.

Weapons That Wait is a recent publication that provides a good summary history of mine warfare. Rommel in Normandy is a history of General Erwin Rommel's preparation for the Allied invasion in Normandy. This is the only work in English that addresses counter-amphibious mining in any detail. As briefly discussed in Chapter One , it was a matter of obvious interest for the German High Command.

Literature pertaining to the case studies varies considerably. Gallipoli is very well documented due to its historical significance. The major figures of Gallipoli, Sir Ian Hamilton and Liman Van Sanders both published diaries shortly after the end of World War I. These publications are essential to any understanding of this complex operation. The Turkish General Staff has also published a history of its actions during this time.

In almost every case all authors writing about Gallipoli understand the effects of the mines used there and cover them adequately. The entire operation, from both military and naval aspects, is very well documented and easy to research.

Normandy is likewise well covered in the literature. For an understanding of the enormity of the naval effort it is necessary to consult Morison's epic work, *United States Naval Operations in World War II*. The problems on the German side are well covered in Ruge's *Rommel in Normandy*. The previously mentioned works on minesweeping both cover the Normandy operation in detail, focusing on the unique problems of assault minesweeping.

The Korean operations are well covered in official CINCPACFLT interim evaluation reports and by the USMC official histories. The Wonsan operation is covered in detail in both sources, which should be considered complimentary. Lott's work, *A Most Dangerous Sea*, ends with a discussion of Wonsan. The sources generally corroborate each other.

Information on Operation Desert Storm is drawn from the articles which have appeared since its conclusion, my personal recollections, and the interview of an officer involved in the mine clearance effort. The works published to date on these operations are contradictory, and in some instances, considerably at variance with the facts. I have used some information from <u>Desert Victory</u> which I personally know to be accurate, however. Desert Storm writings must be approached with care until the historical data can be properly handled.

As ever, the <u>Janes</u> series are comprehensive sources of data both on force size and composition, and technical details of particular weapons. <u>The Dictionary of American Naval Fighting Ships</u> provides additional data on the American mine force and should be regarded as an excellent supplement to Janes.

Trade journals, particularly <u>International Defense Review</u>, are an excellent source of technical data on the various facets of mine warfare. These magazines have a European focus, and most European navies demonstrate a continuing committment to mine warfare vice the cyclical swings of the USN. The depth and currency of this literature is sufficient to allow a reader to keep current with the pace of technology and provides a means to compare U.S. and European initiatives in the field.

Military periodicals, particularly the <u>United States Naval Institute Proceedings</u> and the <u>Marine Corps Gazette</u>, provide the bulk of historical and tactical writings on mine warfare. These articles are in large part historical, depicting the authors contribution to a particular operation or providing an analysis of a particular event as seen from the authors viewpoint. The remainder are tactical, describing a particular threat or describing the tactics and techniques of mine warfare.

These articles are largely written by naval officers, the majority of which had recent mine warfare experience at the time of writing. As previously mentioned, the articles tend to be grouped around particular periods of time when mining activity was significant.

The articles in these professional journals provide a window into the depth of tactical and technical knowledge at the time. The earliest works are often quite lengthy and dwell on the technical characteristics of the mines, and the practical difficulties faced by the mariners who laid and swept them. World War One was the U.S. Navy's first great excursion into mine warfare and the immediate postwar literature of the early 1920's are simply "lessons learned". The Naval Institute Proceedings have often functioned as a public forum for such lessons, especially in earlier years when no official vehicle was in place for the promulgation of such information.

The "nuts and bolts" nature of these early articles is also due to the junior rank of the writers, the majority of which were Lieutenant Commanders or junior. These personnel tended, in that age, to be preoccupied with the technical details of the profession, natural given the nature of their education at the United States Naval Academy and the nature of their daily duties. A strategic analysis of the North

Sea Barrage is nowhere to be found, although the literature abounds with anecdotal stories of its emplacement and later removal.

The professional literature is quiescent during the 1930's. This decade found the Navy concerned with the assimilation of the aircraft carrier and the fleet submarine. The great airpower debates were raging and the battleship versus aircraft carrier controversy was beginning. The Marine Corps was developing the amphibious doctrine it was to use in World War II and the Navy was evaluating its ability to support this doctrine. Mine warfare had been relegated to what was then its primary role of harbor defense. There were few mine craft in commission and few officers assigned to the mission. Those that were so assigned were evidently not inclined to write about it.

After the end of World War II interest in mine warfare at all levels in the Navy appeared to accelerate. The experience of the thousands of sailors who were assigned minesweeping duties was reflected in the literature. For the first time the junior officers writing these articles began to attempt an analyses beyond the technical. The success of Operation Starvation and Operation Paukenshlag impressed the officers who were assigned to evaluate them and a number of superb articles are found in Proceedings from 1945-1950. A number of these pieces were written by intelligence officers who were assigned to debrief Japanese and German commanders.

The Marine Corps had not been severly effected by sea mines in any of its World War II operations. They were, however, nearly always present to some degree and thus were a factor meriting consideration. The primary threat in the Pacific were friendly minefields (possibly one of the great oxymorons of military terminology) which had to be swept before beaches could be reached. At Guadalcanal the SS President Coolidge carrying 5050 troops and heavy weapons was sunk in such a "friendly minefield."[1]

They did amass a great deal of experience dealing with land mines on the beaches and in the shallows, and found these to be as vexing then as they are today. A senior Marine officer lamented,

> The present day mine problem is one of the greatest headaches faced by future amphibious operations. From the four fathom line inward, experts are baffled by the problem at present but are undoubtedly seeking a solution. Unless we can completely isolate the landing areas the Pacific war style of mine clearance cannot be utilized.[2]

The Pacific style of clearance referred to by LTCOL Carter involved the use of combat swimmers and small minesweeping boats as close to the beach as possible. This is possible only when the enemy can be isolated from the

---

[1] Lott, 78.

[2] Donald H. Carter, "Mines-An Amphibious Threat", *Marine Corps Gazette*, 32 (Dec 1948) 40-43.

beachhead and prevented from engaging these units with direct fire.

The mine warfare debacles of the Korean War occasioned a significant amount of professional writing. These articles, written at all levels of the heirarchy, demonstrate the concern over our initial failures in the area. The need to organize and train assault minesweeping elements was again recognized. The first mention of the helicopter as a mine warfare asset is found in a 1951 article.[3] Most importantly, the highest levels of the Navy became aware of the significance of the mine warfare threat.

From the mid 1950's to the early 1970's the literature is once again nearly devoid of writing on the subject. The Navy was focused on the introduction of nuclear power and the assumption of a strategic deterrance role via the fleet ballistic missile submarine program. Mine warfare was not a large problem in the Vietnam War and the majority of efforts were undertaken by the special operations forces. However, the mining of Haiphong and its subsequent clearance via airborne methods sparked a number of articles. These are primarily technical in nature, dealing with the practical problems encountered in planning and conducting this rather large operation. There are several good overviews,

---

[3] E.L. Barker, "The Helicopter in Combat", United States Naval Institute Proceedings, 77 (Nov 1951): 1209.

including one by its commander[4] This operation and the clearance of the Suez Canal provide the bulk of the data found between 1955 and 1986. From 1986 to the present the bulk of the professional literature concerns experiences in the Persian Gulf, both from Operation Earnest Will and Desert Shield/Storm. The Earnest Will literature again deals with the problems of organization, deployment, and operations as the threat was small and the weapons used of obsolete design. Data from Desert Shield/Storm is still pending analysis and that writing which has appeared to date has been largely of the "I told you so" variety.

A significant primary source are the Commander in Chief, U.S. Pacific Fleet Interim Evaluation Reports for the Korean War. These document, issued quarterly for the duration of the conflict, are divided into various naval warfare areas including mine and amphibious warfare. They evaluate the state of training, organization, staff adequacy, intelligence, planning, and tactics and techniques.

Each provides an analysis of the successes and failures of that particular quarter including descriptions of operations and lessons learned. Conclusions are drawn based on the evidence and, where appropriate, recommendations are presented.

---

[4] Brian McCauley, "Operation End Sweep", United States Naval Institute Proceedings, 100 (Mar 1974): 19-25.

Doctrinal publications to be used in the course of the research include JCS Publication 3-02 Amphibious Operations, and the Naval Warfare Publication series for mine warfare and amphibious operations. These publications have remained unchanged in their basic form for many years. JCS Pub 3-02 incorporates the basic amphibious doctrine used by the Navy and Marine Corps and represents an effort to ensure commonality of doctrine. The NWP are Navy specific and thus not subject to pre-emption by joint doctrine. These are technical publications which are useful when extracting the tactics, techniques, and procedures involved in mine countermeasures.

Chapter Three

Methods and Procedures

The thesis and its eventual conclusions will be based on a compilation of historical data and a comparison of this historical data to current conditions. The delimitation of 1914 is necessary as it represents the earliest of a mine-influenced amphibious operation

The study will examine four major operations, Gallipoli, Normandy, Wonsan, and the amphibious portion of Operation Desert Storm, examining the effect of mining upon each and further examining the effect of mine countermeasures upon surprise. This will be done by comparing the size of the mine sweeping problem to the size of the mine sweeping fleet committed to a given operation, and comparing the time required for mine sweeping to the enemy reaction. The mine countermeasures and amphibious forces involved will be drawn from available source documentation. For total force comparisons at various times the data from that years <u>Janes Fighting Ships</u> will be used. The effect of changing technology, i.e. influence fuzing, will be considered in those cases where it is determined to be applicable.

Examination of the data should yield a series of simple relationships that will show the effect of technology upon clearance time, force totals upon clearance time, and clearance time upon surprise. I will attempt to identify those instances where surprise was lost but the effect was negligible due to other factors. An example being the isolation of an amphibious objective area by airpower of naval gunfire. The preponderance of data will be historical, extracted from research and information derived from interviewing officers experienced in the field. After establishing the relationships discussed above I will attempt to determine if the over-riding factor in minefield clearance speed is sheer numbers of sweep assets vice level of technology, and I will examine the effects of various levels of mine sophistication upon clearance speed. Given the assumption that surprise is inversely proportional to the time devoted to mine countermeasures. I will them examine the timelines required for U.S. forces to clear a brigade sized amphibious operating area to determine if those times are excessive.

CHAPTER FOUR
CASE STUDIES IN MINE WARFARE

Introduction

Amphibious warfare, the sudden strike from the sea that surprises an enemy, upsets his plans, and potentially changes a war or campaign in a single stroke, has been a tool of military strategists since man first took to the water. Before the advent of the airborne operation it was the only tool available for such a strike which did not entail long marches , exposure to detection, and expenditure of large amounts of scarce resources. With some very specific exceptions, the nautical phase of the amphibious operation is not affected by terrain. Water is flat and featureless, offering few restrictions to movement and conferring no advantage to the defender. The approach can be made in stealth with the attack falling at any point upon the coastline, and the forces are not exhausted by the effort of getting to the battle area.

Any nation having a littoral is subject to amphibious invasion. Coastline length often exceeds theat of land borders by several times and an irregular coastline such as Norway's or the East Coast of the United States can add thousands of miles of exposure. The problem is analogous to that faced by law enforcement, there are simply too many places which must be watched by too few people.

The flexibility and utility of amphibious warfare is counterbalanced by its vulnerability in several areas. The combat power of a landing force is initially very weak and the success of such an operation hinges upon a rapid buildup of military muscle on the beach. This must be done quickly, before an enemy can react and focus his forces against the beachhead, and it must be done in as benign an environment as possible. Therefore, it is almost axiomatic that amphibious assaults should be conducted against lightly defended areas or in areas where the attacker can quickly develop a decisive positive force ratio. These areas must be isolated from the defenders until sufficient combat power is massed to overcome them.

The amphibious assault initially requires extensive fire support. This support has traditionally come from ships assigned for that purpose, and from the aircraft of the Marine Air Wings. This must continue until the landing force has established its organic fire support means in the objective area. Naval guns can deliver a high volume of fire but must be able to range the beach, generally require observer assistance, and the ships need freedom of maneuver, particularly if a significant counterbattery threat exists. Air support is dependant on a variety of factors, not the least being weather, and generally requires the same level of observation as naval gunfire.

Amphibious assaults are very sensitive to disruptions in timing and synchronization. The right men and material must reach the beach at the critical time if the momentum of the assault is to be maintained. Assaults are normally conducted in waves or serials, and the disruption of any one causes a ripple effect in all following. These ripples can severely disrupt assault timing and result in poorly timed delivery of preparatory fires, beach congestion, and a loss of assault momentum.

Despite these limitations this option continues to be a favorite of strategic and operational planners. It has featured in all recent wars to a greater or lesser degree and its use has become a trademark for some commanders. A successful amphibious operation can yield results completely out of proportion to the resources and effort expended. Similarly, a failed amphibious assault can produce a disaster of like dimension.

The true heart of naval warfare is the inherent mobility of the forces and the mine is the answer to that mobility. Minefields become the terrain of the nautical landscape, and can be used by the defender to impose parameters upon the amphibious threat. The minefields now become the "No-Go" or "Slo-Go" areas familiar to military staff officer, the gaps and lanes in the fields become avenues of approach, and suddenly the threat is considerably diminished and eminently more predictable.

A nation which feels threatened by attack from the sea can achieve economies of force by employing mines. By establishing protective fields, and focusing sensors and weapons systems upon these fields a good degree of protection can be achieved with relatively few forces.

These fields are obstacles in the purest sense and must be breached by any force attempting to pass through them. As on land this breaching process takes time, that most critical and unrecoverable resource. The time spent in breaching a minefield will be used by an alert enemy to analyze the assault, mass forces for the defense, and if the beachhead cannot be isolated then the assault will likely fail.

The four case studies which follow will examine the effect of the mine upon the amphibious assault. I will explore how they were used, how the attacking forces approached the problem of breaching, and most importantly, what their effect was upon the operation.

GALLIPOLI

Gallipoli is to amphibious warfare what Cambrai is to the cavalryman, the first testing of modern techniques and equipment applied to an ancient problem. In the case of Gallipoli that test was to fail in the blood of over half a million men, blood which was shed in large part because less than 500 mines caused a vital loss of surprise.

Any discussion of this operation first requires some explanation of the circumstances which bought the young British, Anzac, and Turkish soldiers to this bleak peninsula in European Turkey. The great German assault in August 1914 had stalled against the defenses of the Anglo-French Entente and both sides had begun to settle into what would become the murderous positional warfare of the Western Front.

In the south as the war began, the entry of Turkey on the side of the Central Powers was by no means assured. Turkey was not threatened by any of the protagonists, had no existing treaty obligations, and had no particular need to go to war. Both the Allies and the Central Powers hoped that she would remain neutral.[1]

Turkey was, in any case, in poor condition to fight enemies such as Great Britain or France. For a hundred

---

[1] Alan Moorehead, *Gallipoli*, (New York: Harper and Row, 1956), 11.

years prior to 1914, the Ottoman empire had been derisively known as the "sick man of Europe". As is the case with many sick men, a large body of interested relatives had gathered around the sickbed, waiting for the demise and the eventual probate of the estate. Much of this estate was gone, Salonika, Crete, and the Aegean Islands to the Greeks, Egypt and Cyprus to Great Britain, and Bulgaria to its own independence.[2]

Turkey had tried, not always successfully, to engage in treaties and alliances with the powers of Europe but was generally rebuffed. Her reputation for misrule, corruption, and cruelty had so alienated the major European powers that they were unwilling to treat with her, and her crumbling and failing state made it unnecessary that they do so. But, as war approached, this frog suddenly began to appear princelike.[3]

For Turkey was cursed by geography to lie at the crossroads of empire. Occupying the northeastern Mediterranean littoral, and extending east to Iraq she sat athwart the major lines of communication between Britain and her empire, and controlled access to the Balkans via the Black Sea. In July 1914, the Germans suddenly became acutely aware of the Black Sea and its importance. They

---

[2] Morehead, 11.

[3] Barbara Tuchman, *The Guns of August* (New York: Macmillan, 1962), 163.

sought to resurrect an offer of alliance previously made by the Turks but left dangling. Negotiations were brought to fruition on July 28, 1914, when the Turks formally requested a secret alliance with the Central Powers following the Austrian declaration of war on Serbia.[4]

Still, this situation could have been salvaged but for a foolish and arrogant move on the part of the British. The Turks had contracted and paid for two battleships, the Sultan Osman and the Reshadieh, to be built in British yards and delivered in the summer of 1914. The money, over thirty million dollars, had been raised by popular subscription from the Turkish population and tremendous national pride was invested in their acquisition. Using a variety of subterfuges, the British delayed the departure of the vessels from May until July, when Winston Churchill, as First Lord of the Admiralty, ordered them requisitioned. No compensation or repayment was offered.[5] The Turks signed an alliance with Germany the day they received notification of the British action.

However, after signing a treaty with Germany whereby they undertook to declare war on Russia and close the Dardanelles, the Turks then failed to do these things. The Turks feared Russia, resented England, and mistrusted

---

[4] Tuchman, 164.

[5] Tuchman, 165.

Germany, and were not at all sure they had backed the right horse. They thus opted to sit out the opening battles of the war to see which way the wind was likely to blow. They were allowed this luxury for slightly over one week.[6]

Two German warships, SMS Goeben and SMS Breslau, were cruising the Mediterranean when war broke out in Europe. These vessels inaugurated the war by shelling the Algerian ports of Bone and Phillipeville, after which they set course for the eastern Mediterranean with the Royal Navy in pursuit. After some equivocation by the Turks and some tactical miscalculation by the Royal Navy, the ships were allowed to enter the Dardanelles on August 10th, 1914.

In a transparent attempt to preserve Turkish neutrality, the ships were commissioned into the Turkish Navy as the Jawus and the Midilli. The German crews remained, donning red fezzes to signify their change of allegiance.[7]

For three months the ships sat idle in the port of Istanbul, then, on October 28th the ships attacked the Russian ports of Odessa, Sevastopal, and Feodosiya. This attack was carried out without the sanction of the Turkish government, and they attempted to disavow it without success. On November 4th, Russia declared war on Turkey, followed the next day by France and Great Britain.[8]

---

[6] Tuchman. 165.

[7] Tuchman. 185.

[8] Tuchman. 187.

Turkey's frantic attempts at disavowal were not without reason. The country was in absolutely no condition to fight, the efforts of Enver Pasha and the "Young Turks" notwithstanding. The Germans had established a military mission in 1913 to train the Turks, and had achieved considerable progress. Nevertheless, the series of Balkan Wars of independence prior to 1914 had drained and expended the Ottoman Army. Excepting only a few elite units, this army had gone unpaid for months, and some units were reportedly on the verge of mutiny.[9] This army was barely ready to maintain order within its domains, and was not prepared to challenge the great powers of Europe. However, with the assistance of the German Military Mission under the command of General Liman Von Sanders, it was to prove adequate to the task.

The months of October, November, and December went by quietly, marked by only a few incidents. The Turks sallied forth two small expeditions, one aimed at the Russian Caucasus, and the other at Egypt, and Allied warships patrolling the entrance to the Dardanelles shelled the forts guarding the mouth of the straits.[10] The British submarine B11 entered the straits on December 13th and sank the

---

[9] Moorehead, 11.

[10] Moorehead, 33.

Turkish battleship Messudieh. These were all local actions, not part of any larger strategic or operational plan.

In Europe the trenches now extended from the North Sea to Switzerland, and the antagonists had already suffered over a million casualties. The British, long intrigued by the operational possibilities of a thrust into central Europe through the Balkans, began to reexamine some long discarded plans for a naval assault on Istanbul. This appeared to offer relief for the Russians, who had suffered from the disastrous battles at Tannenburg and the Masurian Lakes, would knock Turkey out of the war, and would divert German forces from the Western Front, thus offering some possibility for decisive action.[11] This thinking was bolstered by a Russian request in late December inquiring if some sort of action against the Turks could be undertaken to relieve pressure in the Caucasus.[12]

This request was taken by the British with some reluctance. While the plight of the Russians was recognized, and the operational value of such a move was accepted, a body of the Imperial General Staff felt the request would divert precious resources from the Western Front, and thus could not be honored. This view was briefly supported by the Secretary of War, Lord Kitchener, but a

---

[11] Moorehead, 35.

[12] Moorehead, 35.

review of the Russian condition caused him to change his position regarding the need for such an operation. He would not, however, agree to commit any ground troops.[13]

This thrust the burden of the action onto the Admiralty, under the leadership of the First Lord, Winston Churchill, and the First Sea Lord, Fleet Admiral Sir John (Jackie) Fisher.[14] They envisioned a forcing of the straits by battleships which would bombard Istanbul and force Turkish capitulation. This had nearly occurred in 1807 when a British admiral had sailed to within eight miles of the city before losing the wind and being forced to retire.[15] This they proposed to do using a squadron of battleships of the Majestic and Canopus classes. These were obsolete ships whose armament was inadequate for a sea battle with the German High Seas Fleet but perfectly suitable for destroying the antique forts guarding the straits. Vice Admiral Sackville-Carden, commanding the squadron blockading the Dardanelles, was tasked to prepare such a plan.

He responded promptly on 11 January 1915, stating his opinion that such a plan was feasible and laying out his

---

[13] Moorehead, 36.

[14] Fisher was a highly opinionated, irascible, and forceful man who had participated in the moderization of the Royal Navy at the turn of the century. He was returned to active duty and elevated to the peerage at the beginning of the war. He is one of the notable characters of the Royal Navy, pugnacious, irreverant, and driven.

[15] Moorehead, 36.

force requirements. These were: 12 battleships, 3 battle cruisers, 3 light cruisers, 1 flotilla leader, 16 destroyers, 6 submarines, 4 seaplanes, and 12 minesweepers. The plan was exceedingly simple, to demolish the Turkish forts by indirect battleship gunfire, and then to sail up the straits led by the minesweepers. The plan was rapidly approved by the Admiralty, with the only major change being the addition of the new battleship Queen Elizabeth.[16] The French agreed to augment this force with four battleships and their auxiliaries. With this assistance from the Allies, and after quelling some last minute arguments within the Admiralty, the necessary orders were issued to set the plan in motion.

EUROPEAN SIDE	ASIAN SIDE
30 Heavy Guns	31 Heavy Guns
6 Medium guns	8 Medium Guns
3 Medium Howitzers	4 Medium Howitzers[18]

Figure Seven

To understand what happened during the course of the naval attacks it is necessary to understand the geography of the Dardanelles. The straits are forty miles long,

---

[16] Moorehead. 39.

[17] Sherman Miles, "Notes on the Dardanelles Campaign of 1915", undated reprint from The Coastal Artillery Journal. 11.

stretching from Cape Helles on the Mediterranean to the Black Sea. They average approximately four miles in width, except at one point fourteen miles above Cape Helles, where they narrow to three quarters of a mile. This point, the Narrows, is critical to control of the Dardanelles, and becomes the key choke point in the campaign.[17] The Turks had been fortifying the straits for many years and a variety of forts, guns and barriers were in place to prevent uninvited naval excursions. Figure six depicts armaments in the Narrows.

Of these guns six were fourteen inch naval rifles, purpose built for coastal defense. The remainder were military weapons designed for land warfare. This weight of fire covered a waterway less than a mile in width.

These large weapons are difficult to fire from fixed positions at moving targets so the Turkish had designed a method to slow ships and expose them to the overwatching fires for a longer period. Beginning approximately three miles south of the Narrows the Turks laid 344 moored contact mines in eleven lines. These mine lines did not completely cross the straits, but were staggered to create a torturous clear channel.[19] Any ship attempting to clear the minefields was exposed to the fire of the shore

---

[18] Moorehead. 52.

[19] Robert Rhodes James, *Gallipoli*, (New York: Macmillian, 1965), 15.

batteries, and any ship maneuvering to engage the shore batteries was exposed to the mines.

The Allied forces began the action on the morning of February 19, 1915, with an attack on the forts guarding the Dardanelles entrance. The ships were arranged by Admiral Carden into three divisions as shown in figure seven.

HMS Inflexible	HMS Vengeance	Suffren
HMS Agamemmnon	HMS Albion	Bouvet
HMS Queen Elizabeth	HMS Cornwallis	Charlemagne
	HMS Irresistible	Gaulois
	HMS Triumph[20]	

Figure Eight

The attack was to occur in three parts, three bombardments at ever decreasing ranges, preceded by minesweepers which would clear the channel leading to the strait. The first day results were mixed. Ships of that day did not have continuous aiming fire control systems and the guns had to be relaid optically each time they were fired. They were therefore not especially accurate at long ranges and failed to completely reduce the forts.

---

[21] Moorehead, 55.

Accordingly, it was decided to close the range and engage the forts with direct point blank fire.[21]

This was done on February 25th with better results. Cardens second in command, Vice Admiral De Robeck, led an attack right into the mouth of the straits, engaged the forts, and landed armed shore parties to capture the facilities and destroy the enemy guns. The shore parties were essentially unopposed, and the Turks abandoned their fortifications at the mouth of the Dardanelles. The minesweepers swept for six miles into the straits, found no mines, and returned. They reported difficulty making way against the southerly current, a problem which was to surface again later.[22]

Other problems had begun to surface with the Gallipoli mine sweeping force, which then numbered thirty five, twenty-one of which were British, and fourteen French. The British sweepers in use were North Sea fishing trawlers, taken up from trade with their crews, and rigged with a crude minesweeping system. They were not under naval discipline, but were simply contracted to perform the function. The Turks, recovering from the attacks of 25 Feb, had begun to move and hide their mobile batteries. The minesweepers, working at night to sweep the Narrows,

---

[20] Moorehead, 55.

[22] Moorehead, 56.

found themselves constantly illuminated by searchlights and exposed to harassing fire.[23] The dilemma of Gallipoli was making itself felt. the minesweepers could not remove the mines until the guns were suppressed. and the guns could not be suppressed until the mines were swept.

The crews of the minesweepers felt that it was simply too much. In the words on one of their officers.

> "The men recognized sweeping risks and did not mind being blown up, but they hated the gunfire, and pointed out that they were not supposed to sweep under fire, they had not joined for that".[24]

This naturally infuriated the officers of the Royal Navy who were charged with seeing the action through. Captain Roger Keyes, Chief of Staff to Carden, called for volunteers from the RN, and offered the civilian crews a bonus for another try at the mines. On March 10, 1915, under Keyes' leadership, the flotilla again attempted to sweep to the Narrows. The searchlights again illuminated the force, and the Turkish batteries began a duel with the minesweepers and their supporting battleship, HMS Canopus. The attempt was a failure. Rattled by the fire the sweepers struck mines and failed to deploy their equipment properly.[25] Another attempt the following night met with like results. The crews of the

---

[23] Moorehead. 57.

[24] Moorehead. 57.

[25] Moorehead. 59.

minesweepers were not trained for the task at hand and lacked the resolution to carry it through.

By March 13th, new crews had been assembled for the flotilla, and Captain Keyes was ready to try it again. This time the force swept mines under concentrated Turkish fire until all but three of the force had been put out of action. A large number of mines were cut free and exploded the following day. The commander, encouraged by the positive results, scheduled the full scale naval assault for 17 or 18 March.[26]

To lose all but three of an attacking force would hardly seem a positive result, but the minesweepers were regarded as expendable by the Admiralty. Churchill, on March 14th, sent the following cable to Carden.

> "I do not understand why minesweepers should be interfered with by firing which causes no casualties. Two or three hundred casualties would be a moderate price to pay for sweeping up as far as the Narrows . . . This work has to be done whatever the loss of life and small craft and the sooner it is done the better".[27]

March 18th dawned sunny and calm, and the Allied fleet under Admiral de Robeck prepared to assault the straits.[28] The fleet was arranged in three divisions comprised of

---

[26] Moorehead. 60.

[27] Moorehead. 59.

[28] De Robeck had relieved Carden on March 15th after Carden was diagnosed as being on the verge of nervous collapse. Moorehead. 61.

battleships and battle cruisers, with the British in the lead. The minesweeping flotilla was stationed outside the straits with orders to enter when the guns had been silenced. The planners envisaged that the channel would be open by that evening, and that the battleships would proceed to Istanbul the following day.[29]

At 11:35 a.m. the assault began with Queen Elizabeth, Agamemmnon, Lord Nelson, and Inflexible engaging the forts at Chanak and Kilid Bahr which guarded the Narrows. The ships bombarded the forts until slightly after noon when the French battleships were called forward to carry out the close range attack on the inner defenses. This they did with vigor, and by 1:45 p.m. the Turkish fire had practically ceased.[30]

The French were then ordered to retire, and De Robeck ordered up the remaining division from outside the straits. As the French departed down the south side of the straits, through Eren Keui Bay, the battleship Bouvet struck a mine. Traveling at high speed she capsized and sank within two minutes, taking down 640 men.[31] At this the Turkish gunners reengaged, but were again battered into submission, falling silent by 4:00 p.m. The minesweepers were called up,

---

[29] Moorehead, 62.

[30] Moorehead, 64.

[31] Moorehead, 65.

sweeping three mines, but they panicked when fired upon by the Turkish light batteries, and fled the scene.

Shortly thereafter, HMS Inflexible struck a mine near where Bouvet had sunk, and retired with heavy damage and casualties. Her sister ship, Irresistible, was next. Striking a mine in the same vicinity and losing power, she was taken under heavy fire by the Turks as she drifted inshore. HMS Ocean followed suit, and by nightfall the Allies had lost one battleship, had one heavily damaged and retiring, and two crewless and adrift in the Dardanelles.

Keyes, aboard the destroyer HMS Jed, searched throughout the night for Irresistible and Ocean, but both had sunk.[32] The British and French, believing that they had located all the minefields, were at a loss to explain the losses.

One man gets the credit for this feat. Lieutenant Colonel Geehl, a Turkish coastal defense expert, had taken a small steamer, Nousret, into Eren Keui Bay on March 8th and laid a line of twenty mines. In the intervening ten days the minesweepers found but three, and the Allies did not believe these to be part of a larger field. Aerial reconnaissance had also failed to notice them.[33] Some of these mines were Russian, the Turks having gotten so short on ordnance that they were reduced to collecting mines

---

[32] Moorehead, 69.

[33] Moorehead, 77.

floated down the Black Sea by the Russians in hope of damaging Goeben or Breslau.[34]

Events of the 18th were observed by General Sir Ian Hamilton, the newly appointed commander in chief of the Gallipoli expedition. His was to have been the task of occupying the area when the Turks capitulated, now he realized that the much more difficult task of forced entry lay ahead. The Army must land and silence the guns before the fleet could open the straits and carry the attack to Istanbul.[35]

Keyes, in the meantime, had set about reorganizing the minesweeping fleet to accomplish its mission. He obtained thirty eight powerful trawlers capable of sweeping upstream at fourteen knots, and fitted twenty four destroyers with sweep gear. These he crewed with the survivors of the sunken battleships, sending the craven North Sea crews home. In a short time he had organized an incomparably superior force to that which had started the campaign.[36] Why didn't he use it?

The answer is two fold. The first is that after viewing the naval battle on the 18th, the Army felt that it wasn't necessary and that they could undertake the assault without

---

[34] Moorehead. 76.

[35] Sir Ian Hamilton, *Gallipoli Diary*, (New York: George Doran and Co., 1920), 51.

[36] Miles. 16.

the straits being opened. Hamilton and his staff were concerned over risking the large, expensive ships in the minefields.[37] Secondly, De Robeck had lost his nerve after seeing three capital ships lost in one afternoon. Despite the urgings of Keyes the fleet went to anchor and the splendid minesweeping fleet he assembled would never be used.[38]

The effort the Allies had undertaken and the losses they had suffered did not go unnoticed by General Liman Von Sanders, the head of the German Military Mission and the man who was to conduct the defense of Gallipoli. He offered the following thought:

> " The Allies now realized that the road to Istanbul could not be opened by action on the water alone. It was equally clear to me that they would not relinquish such a high prize without further effort . . . Hence, a large landing had to be counted upon."[39]

Thus the element of surprise was lost, and from that point on it was a race between the Allies and the Turks. Instead of being a surprise, the campaign was telegraphed as few have ever been. The object of the effort was now to see if the defenders could fortify faster than the invaders could assemble combat power ashore.

---

[37] Hamilton. 41.

[38] Moorehead. 89.

[39] Liman Von Sanders, <u>Five Years In Turkey</u>, (Baltimore: Williams and Wilkins, 1928) 56.

On April 25th, the first troops landed at the toe of the Gallipoli peninsula and the battle began which was to last until the eighth of January, 1916. The Allied Navy, shaken by the losses of March 18th, refused to employ the larger and more capable forces they assembled. The Allied forces piled ashore, only to be held just inland of the beaches by the Turkish defenders. The following comment summarizes the position of the naval forces:

> "The peninsula was now for us little better than a bottomless pit: swallowing all the men and munitions we could throw into it. The Navy was left helpless off the beach with no more useful duty than to supply the needs of the Army, and protect it as far as the restricted use of its gun power permitted"[40]

Later in the campaign plans were made to have the fleet proceed up the strait, interdict the roads supplying the Turks, and attack the rear of their positions at Bulair on the neck of the peninsula. Such an operation might well have broken the resolve of the defenders and allowed the Allies to break out of their beach head.[41] This operation never came to pass for the same reason that it had failed previously, the guns protecting the minefields could not be silenced, and without this precaution, the minesweepers could not proceed.

---

[40] C.O. Head, _A Glance at Gallipoli_, (London: Eyre and Spottiswoode, 1931) 136.

[41] Hamilton, 215.

In January 1916 the Allied forces were evacuated from the Gallipoli peninsula in an operation that went as well as all the previous had gone wrong. The Allies suffered 252,000 casualties out of 489,000 committed, the Turks 251,309 casualties out of 500,000 committed; rates of 51 and 50 percent respectively.[42] That these casualties were so high was due, in large part, to the mine warfare efforts of the Turkish Army.

The failure was due to several factors. First among these was technology. The mines in use by the Turks were moored contact mines of a type developed by the Russians in 1908 which were set to float at a predetermined depth. This depth is arrived at by computing the range of the tide, the average draft of your targets, and setting the length of the mooring cable to cover this range. These mines are easily swept by towing an underwater device through the minefield designed to snag or cut these cables. The mine, being positively buoyant, then rises to the surface and is destroyed by gunfire. The minesweepers, naturally, must be of shallower draft than the mines they are sweeping. This was not the case at Gallipoli, and four of the craft were lost in the fields.[43] The sweep gear was primitive, as the Oropesa sweep, which was to become the standard means for

---

[42] Moorehead, 361.

[43] James, 49.

removing this type of mine, was still in development. These minefields, and the Allied countermeasures, represented the peak of mine warfare technology available at the time.

Training was an equal cause of the failure. The crews of the minesweepers, contracted fishermen, were not prepared to conduct a clearance operation under fire. They had been hired for what they regarded as a large explosive ordnance disposal operation and were unwilling to attempt this opposed. Royal Navy crews and officers should have been assigned this task from the beginning.

The final, and most significant failure, was the failure of nerve on the part of the senior commander, Vice Admiral John De Robeck. By the time the Army landed the minesweeping flotilla was larger, better trained, and better equipped than at any point previous. Nonetheless, he forswore the attempt despite the urgings of his chief of staff and the long distance chiding of Churchill. The events of March 18th had demonstrated that the Turkish guns at the Narrows could be silenced by naval gunfire, and that being the case, the mines could be swept and the passage to Istanbul opened. This failure, more than any other, accounts for the tragedy of Gallipoli.

The subordinate thesis questions can be answered as follows:

Q. Does the loss of tactical surprise make a large scale amphibious assault unfeasible?

A. In this case, yes. The minesweeping efforts and the naval assault on the Narrows alerted General Von Sanders that something was afoot. Only a cursory analysis was required to arrive at the fact that an amphibious assault was forthcoming. The details of the defense were relatively simple to a trained professional land forces officer.

Q. Based on historical data, what level of losses can be expected by amphibious forces entering a mined area.

A. In this case three ships were sunk and one seriously damaged attempting to force the fields.

Q. What level of mine clearance effort is required to sweep an amphibious operating area for a large scale assault.

A. Gallipoli yields little data regarding this question. The 344 mines were arranged in eleven lines perpendicular to the shore, cutting a channel through such a field is not particularly difficult. Additionally, the moored contact mine is swept by cutting its cable, so a single pass through such a field removes all mines at or above the depth of the sweep gear.

Q. Would the sweep effort alert the enemy to potential landing areas.

A. At Gallipoli, the effort alerted the enemy that a landing was probable. Because of the geography of the peninsula, it was unnecessary to know the exact landing beach. Von Sanders had merely to stage forces down the peninsula and isolate the Allied beach heads as they were established.

Q. What level of losses can be expected by the mine clearance forces.

A. In this case all but four of thirty five minesweepers were lost or damaged while sweeping. The majority of these losses were to the overwatch fires and not to the mines themselves. This represents a casualty rate of 88.5 %.

Q. Would expected losses render an amphibious assault force combat ineffective.

A. In this case, no. The amphibious transport used for Gallipoli numbered over 200 ships, the Turks had deployed 344 mines. To achieve a 30% reduction in the force the mines would have to sink 60 ships. The minesweepers did not have to remove all of these mines, only sufficient numbers to allow navigation. This involves sweeping and marking a narrow channel through the minelines. There were eleven lines, each of thirty one mines, crossing a 1750 yard channel. 1750/31= a spacing of 56.4 yards per mine, the removal of three mines per line, 33 mines, would clear a channel 169.2 yards wide, adequate even for modern shipping. Had the transports sailed into the mine lines it is unlikely that they would have even struck a mine, given the large spacing between them.

Q. Are current minesweeping techniques adequate to clear an amphibious operation area in a timely manner.

A. In this case they were. Provided the paravane was set at the proper depth every mine encountered would be swept. The area swept to one side of a minesweeper using this technique is normally 200 yards. Three minesweepers, with 50% overlap, would sweep a 400 yard wide channel. At a sweep speed of five knots a channel through the entire Dardanelles could have been swept in eight hours.

Q. How does mine technology affect the duration of a minesweeping operation.

A. At Gallipoli, the mines were of two types, moored with a contact fuze, or command detonated. There was no recorded use of any type of sweep obstruction device. The mine technology was familiar and understood by both sides, as were the appropriate countermeasures. There was no appreciable affect due to technology.

NORMANDY

World War I provided a plethora of lessons in mine warfare to those who took notice. The United States and Great Britain laid the great North Sea mine barrage in an attempt to obstruct the passage of the German U Boats into the Atlantic. Gallipoli had shown that this simple device could render an overwhelming naval force ineffective. Over all things, war is the crucible of technology, and by the end of the war the belligerants had begun to develop the more sophisticated devices which would plague and please the sailors of World War II.

First among these was the magnetically actuated mine. These mines use the variation in the earths magnetic field caused by the proximity of a large ferrous ships hull to move a needle, closing a circuit and detonating the primary charge. These weapons are sensitive to a number of influences such as the differing magnetic field strength at differing latitudes, represent considerable engineering effort, and are an order of magnitude more complex than the simple contact mines they supplemented. These mines are negatively buoyant and lie on the bottom waiting for their targets. Thus they cannot be swept by cutting devices, but rather require either actuation of their fuzes or location and destruction by divers. Great Britian, Germany, and the

United States had all developed crude versions of these by the close of hostilities.

Minesweeping had also grown. The British had developed the Oropesa sweep as the standard method of clearing moored mines. This sweep, named after the ship upon which it was first developed, consisted of a single wire which had a torpedo shaped float attached to its outer end. Suspended from this float was a small hydroplane device called the "otter" which veered the sweep wire away from the ship. At the forward end of the wire was a "kite", another hydroplane which determined the sweep depth. Attached along the wire at intervals were explosive cutters designed to sever a mines mooring cable.[44] The Oropesa could be streamed from both sides simultaneously, thus doubling the area a single ship could sweep. A futher advantage of this technique is that minesweepers could now steam in echelon with overlapping sweep coverage. This allowed all sweepers, less the lead ship, to steam in swept water.

New minesweepers had appeared. In the Royal Navy the underpowered fishing trawlers of Gallipoli had been replaced with a fleet of modern minesweepers. Notable among these was the 220 ft Hunt class, coal fired and capable of 10 knot speeds, as well as the larger and more efficient Brigewater, Town, and Halcyon classes. For shallow water work side

---

[44] Peter Elliot, *Allied Minesweeping In World War 2*, (Annapolis: Naval Institute Press, 1979). 29

wheel paddle steamers had been built, capable of sweeping in 6.5 feet of water at nine knots.[45]

The United States had laid many mines during the first World War but had swept relatively few, thus the body of experience and fleet interest was less than that found in the Royal Navy. The Bird class minesweepers of World War I had largely been decommissioned, and the few that remained in service were transferred to the Asiatic Fleet.[46]

The increasing liklihood of hostilities caused the U.S. Navy to contract for the "Raven" class fleet minesweeper in 1938. The first of these 220 foot, steel hulled ships, USS Auk, was delivered on January 15, 1942.[47] Realizing that the Ravens would be delivered nearly four years after their requisitioning, the USN began an emergency requisition of 60 commercial fishing boats to serve as coastal minesweepers. These were commissioned in the winter of 1939-40, becoming a second "Bird" class with such names as Plover, Bunting, and Condor.[48] A class of small 97 foot wooden hulled craft for inshore minesweeping was also ordered. The American minesweepers were initially fitted for single or double

---

[45] Elliot. 18.

[46] Elliot. 69.

[47] Arnold Lott, Most Dangerous Sea, (Annapolis: Naval Institute Press, 1959). 35.

[48] Lott. 33.

Oropesa sweeps and later modified to carry the special equipment needed to sweep the more advanced mines.[49]

The final significant American advance prior to the start of the war was the design of the yard motor minesweeper (YMS). This class of small minesweeper, 561 of which were launched during the war, was to dominate Allied mine clearance operations throughout the conflict.[50]

The major powers had accumulated significant experience in all aspects of mine warfare by the end of World War I. The sweeping operations at Gallipoli, the emplacement and post war removal of the seventy plus thousand mines in the North Sea Barrage, and coastal clearance had produced a large corporate body of knowledge. Unfortunately, this was allowed to rapidly dissipate after 1919.

For reasons previously discussed in this thesis the major navies of the world hold mine warfare in poor regard, and it tends to suffer from neglect between conflicts. In the 1920's and early 1930's the entire U.S. Navy's effort in the field consisted of one physist attached to the Naval Ordnance Laboratory, designing mines which were never produced.[51] The Royal Navy's actions were slightly more robust in that they operated the fleet mine warfare training

---

[49] Elliot. 69.

[50] Lott. 38.

[51] Lott. 17.

school, HMS Vernon, which was to provide the body of technical expertise needed when war erupted.[52]

The Germans had devoted considerable engineering and military effort to developing mine warfare in the 1930's and were ready with a stock of approximately 200,000 moored mines when the war began.[53] As soon as the war was declared German naval units began to lay mines in the Thames Estuary and along the Channel coast. The British responded by requisitioning nearly 800 comercial vessels, outfitting them for minesweeping operations, and sending them to sea.[54]

The story of mine warfare at the Normandy invasion is largely a Royal Navy one. To understand the speed and efficiency with which they swept the invasion areas it is important to understand the depth of experience gained and level of effort they sustained between September 1939 and June 1944. The German efforts and the British parrys continued without letup for the entire war. Both parties developed new weapons and countermeasures constantly, and much of the development in this branch of naval warfare comes from this conflict.

The magnetic mine appeared very early in the fall of 1939. German aircraft had been observed parachuting objects

---

[52] Lott. 18.

[53] Elliot. 30.

[54] Elliot. 30.

into the water, and unexplained explosions were reported in various areas around the coast.[55] Ships began to be sunk or damaged in these areas, without any contact mines being sighted. The Japanese liner Terukuni Maru and the destroyer Gipsy, among others, were seriously damaged in November while operating in the Thames estuary.[56]

On November 22, 1939 the British discovered a German magnetic mine which had been inadvertantly dropped in a mud flat. It was disarmed and removed to HMS Vernon for technical exploitation.[57] After determining the characteristics of the sensor mechanism the British were able to develop a countermeasure which they fielded in January 1940.

This countermeasure initially took the form of a large magnetic coil mounted on a wooden barge and towed by a tugboat. It was followed by the first incidence of airborne mine countermeasures. Wellington bombers were fitted with magnetic coils and flown down channels at wavetop height. Both methods produced results but were not deemed the final answer.[58]

---

[55] These were mines which exploded prematurely, a problem which exists to this day. Elliot. 31.

[56] Lott. 18.

[57] Ellis Johnson and David Thatcher, Mines Against Japan, (Washington D.C., Naval Ordnance Laboratory, 1973). 10.

[58] Elliot. 33.

After some experimentation with various magnetic field generators in trawlers the LL sweep was developed. This sweeping technique involved the towing of two cables astern of the minesweeper which were electrically pulsed. This established a magnetic field which detonated the mine. This basic technique is still in use today.[59]

The advent of the magnetic mine had other effects. The use of steel hulled ships for sweeping was now inadvisable and the construction of wooden hulled vessels was begun. From this point until the early 1970's and the advent of Glass Reinforced Plastic (GRP) all minesweepers were wooden. The techniques of de-perming, a temporary reduction in a ships magnetic field by passing energized cables around it, and degaussing, the installation of cables on or in the hull to achieve a permanent reduction, were developed.[60]

By the summer of 1940 the British had the measure of the magnetic mines then in use. The sweeping totals mounted throughout the summer as more LL equipped units reached the fleet. By October 1940 250 vessels were so equipped and had swept over 900 magnetic mines.[61] Moored mines continued to appear, primarily laid by German surface craft. These mines were equipped with sweep obstructors, devices designed to

---

[59] Elliot. 33.

[60] Elliot. 35.

[61] Elliot. 36.

trigger the mine or damage the sweeping gear. Adaptations to these tactics included strengthing the sweep gear and increasing the stocks of spare equipment. At years end the Royal Navy had swept 1,214 magnetic mines, 767 moored contact mines, and 105 of the new accoustically actuated mines.

The accoustic mine was simply the latest in the technological war between to scientifically inclined enemies. These mines incorporated a simple microphone to capture the vibration made by a passing ships internal machinery. The initial model, first employed in October 1940, was uncomplicated and coarsely set. The coarser the mine setting, the more subject it is to actuation by any sound, rather than one specific to a particular type of ship, and the easier it is to sweep. These mines also employed a six day delay clock which prevented arming for this period. Minesweepers attempting to clear such a field before the mines activated would have no effect.[63]

The solution to sweeping such a mine is simple, introduce a noise of the required frequency and intensity into the water. This actuates the firing mechanism and the mine is thus swept or "lifted". The British had postulated the existance of such devices and prepared countermeasures. The most successful sweep method was using a pneumatic

---
[63] Elliot, 48.

hammer, adapted from an ordinary jack hammer. This noisemaker, designated the SA sweep, was attached to an LL sweep and towed.[64]

The Germans laid a large mixed magnetic/acoustic field in the Thames Estuary on December 12-13. The three minesweepers equipped with SA gear were unequal to the task and seven ships were lost with the channel being closed for four days. This shock galvanized the Admiralty, and by mid-January 1941 224 sets of the equipment were at sea.[65]

By the end of 1941 the British Commonwealth Navies had amassed considerable experience in mine warfare. They had swept a total of 1407 magnetic mines, 992 acoustic mines, and 1042 contact mines. In the process they had lost 97 mine warfare ships of various types, as well as 11 larger warships and 291 merchants, 140 ships of various types had been damaged.[66] To compensate, the minecraft fleet had risen from 76 on 1 Sept 1939 to 971 exactly two years later.

The German weapons had become increasingly more sophisticated as 1941 wore on. They introduced the type G magnetic mine which required a large coarse magnetic flux to fire it. This feature resisted sweeping by the LL equipment, and fired only when large ships actuated it. Two

---

[64] Elliot, 53.

[65] Elliot, 51.

[66] Elliot, 52.

acoustic mines made their appearance, the A.2, featuring increased microphone sensitivity and a 12 actuation delay clock; and the M.A. 1. This mine incorporated the first dual magnetic/acoustic firing unit. An acoustic signature would arm the mine and the magnetic field variation would fire it. This mine caused the adaptation of the dual LL/SA sweep technique.[67]

In the United States the events of 1939 and 1940 were noticed. Two officers were assigned to "mine warfare desks" in the Navy Department, one of these men, CAPT Alexander Sharp, was to figure prominantly in the Pacific mine campaign. An extensive exchange of liaison personnel began, with the USN observing and adopting the various British countermeasures techniques and equipment as they were adapted. One of the liaison officers, Ensign Charles Howard, became the USN's first mine warfare casualty when he was killed attempting to defuse a German magnetic mine.[68] During this same period the USN began to order and install degaussing equipment and to set up deperming stations. As the requisitioned commercial vessels began to be refitted as minesweepers the Naval Mine Warfare School opened at Yorktown, Virginia and graduated its first class in May 1941. In March of that year drill minefields were laid and

---

[67] Elliot. 54.

[68] Lott. 19.

the fleet began to train in earnest to recover some of the skills lost since 1918.[69]

When the United States entered the war those skills rapidly came into demand. The Germans initiated Operation Paukenschlag, the U-Boat campaign off the U.S. East coast. This combination of magnetic and acoustic mines, laid by submarine, was to sink 10 ships for a total of 338 mines laid. The port of New York was closed for two days, the Chesapeake Bay, Jacksonville, and Savannah for three, Wilmington for eight, and Charleston, S.C. for eleven.[70] Clearing the fields already laid and check sweeping occupied the efforts of 125 minesweepers, mostly of the small inshore variety which were beginning to be delivered in sizable numbers. By the end of 1942 210 of these small craft had been delivered, the total would reach 561 by wars end.[71]

Aside from sweeping the Atlantic coast and some small effort in the Pacific, the American mine countermeasures force was only lightly employed in the early years of the war. Operation Torch, the invasion of North Africa, had little mine warfare action.

In 1943 the first major amphibious assaults on Europe began with the invasion of Sicily-Operation Husky. The year

---

[69] Lott. 21.

[70] Lott. 53.

[71] Elliot. 76.

had been a quiet one for the mine warfare forces. mine counts and losses were sharply down in British home waters due to the efforts of the minesweepers and the Royal Air Force. This quiet time had allowed the Allies to concentrate on shipbuilding without suffering excessive attrition. and by July 1943 the forces were raedy to support their first major amphibious assault.

Operation Husky was a three pronged amphibious assault utilizing a task force of 580 ships supported by 24 British and 35 American minesweepers.[72] Despite the rough seas the ships cleared the approach channels. the transport unloading areas. the fire support areas. and the boat lanes leading to the beach. The small YMS (Yard Motor Minesweeper) with its 6.5 foot maximum draft could sweep very close to the beach and proved its utility in this invasion. The forces located only one mine field. not obstructing any of the invasion lanes. but gained invaluable experience in this particular type of minecountermeasures support.[73]

In September 1943 the next large assault in the Mediterannean was conducted. Operation Avalanche. the invasion of the Italian mainland at Salerno. was supported by 13 British and 32 U.S. minesweepers. Intelligence had reported that the Gulf of Salerno was mined. The flotilla

---

[72] Elliot. 85.

[73] Lott. 116.

swept five lanes into the assault beaches, leaving the remainder of the mines in place as a defensive minefield. The flotilla cleared 331 mines and lost no ships to mines. This assault was significant in that it further validated assault sweeping techniques and provided experience in clearing live mines in the amphibious operating areas.[74]

Assault sweeping technique was maturing rapidly by this point. The typical sequence of events would involve an initial fast clearance of the boat lanes by large minesweepers utilizing Oropesa sweeps. They would be lead by smaller launchs conducting a "skim sweep" with light rope sweep gear designed to remove moored mined close to the surface. An influence sweep using LL and SA gear would follow, usually conducted by the shallow draft YMS who would sweep to the minimum depth possible. They would be followed by small boats towing very light sweep gear to clear the very shallow water. Divers would clear inshore of these.[75] After the beach approaches had been cleared the minesweepers would move offshore and begin to sweep the transport unloading areas, fire support areas, and anchorages. This was normal sweeping, made difficult by the large numbers of ships in the areas and the frequent loss of equipment cut

---

[74] Elliot. 86.

[75] Elliot. 92.

free by them.[76] When the assault commenced the minesweepers would withdraw and begin periodic maintenance sweeping.

The final large European assault prior to Normandy was Operation Shingle, the invasion at Anzio. The two assault groups were assigned 41 minesweepers to clear the amphibious operating area. The sweeping was conducted as outlined above, in the now familiar patterns. Three minecraft were lost in lifting 34 mines.[77] Having participated in three large amphibious assaults and fought the Germans in the Atlantic, the mine warfare forces were ready for the largest amphibious operation ever conducted-Operation Overlord.

The Germans had been fortifying the coast of France for some time. General Erwin Rommel, in command of German forces in France had developed a sophisticated and formidable obstacle system to prevent an amphibious assault. Prominant in his calculations was the integration of the sea mine into his obstacle system. Rommel was astute in his choice of a naval advisor, selecting Admiral Freidrich Ruge, an expert in coastal defense and a devotee of mine warfare.

The Germans had been observing British mineing efforts along the French coast and had observed that they did not plant mines in the Bay of the Seine. This area, which includes the Normandy beaches, was correctly assumed to be

---

[76] Elliot, 93.

[77] Lott, 130.

the site of the impending assault. Accordingly, they undertook a concerted minelaying campaign in this area using all types of mines at their disposal.[78] The effect of this effort was diluted by German service politics. The commander of the naval forces in the area, not being an advocate of mine warfare, had not pushed the laying of a maximum number of mines.[79]

The Germans practiced flawless doctrinal employment of mines. Their approach was to lay the mines in belts, moored mines in deeper water, followed by ground mines in the shallower areas. The mines were all equipped with various types of sweep obstructors.[80] In the very shallow areas directly offshore they developed a new type of coastal mine. This device, known as coastal mine A resembled a giant Kewpie doll. The warhead was the weight on the bottom holding the mine upright, extending two meters upward from this was a two meter steel frame topped with a chemical horn contact fuze. When a sweeper struck this mine it merely rolled over, righting itself when the sweep gear was clear.[81] The fields were laid in water as shallow as practicable, both to increase the exposure of the sweepers

---

[78] Friedrich Ruge, <u>Rommel in Normandy</u>, (San Rafael: Presidio Press, 1979.) 38.

[79] Ruge. 175.

[80] Ruge. 38.

[81] Ruge. 20.

to artillery fire, and to cause them to lose their sweep gear in the obstacle-filled shallows.

This was the plan, and plans rarely survive contact with the enemy. The Germans, fooled into believing the invasion was to come at the Pas de Calais, and unable to decide the defense strategy for Festung Europa, never laid the network of mine defenses they planned. This was not known by the Allies, and they planned and executed a minesweeping operation larger and more complex than any previously conducted. Sufficient were laid, particularly in the American sector, to occupy the sweeping forces.

The minesweepers had two tasks, sweeping channels across the English Channel to the amphibious operating area in the Bay of the Seine, and the normal assault sweeping task described above. To accomplish this they assembled a fleet of 385 minesweepers, 35 American and the remainder British or Canadian. This flotilla was assembled shortly before the invasion, and due to the continuous requirement for their services they were unable to assemble and train as a unit prior to the invasion.[82]

The minesweeping plan for Operation Overlord involved several steps. The first was the clearing of channels along the south coast of England. The channels were connected to the major invasion ports and assembly areas, and routed

---

[82] Lott, 185.

thirteen miles offshore to a large cleared circular assembly area. This area was known as area "Z", and nicknamed Picadilly Circus.[83]

Next, ten channels were cut from Area Z across the channel to the amphibious operating area. These channels were marked at their entrances by underwater sonar buoys to provide accurate reference points.[84] There were five invasion task forces, with two channels, 400 yards in width, allocated per force to allow passage of slow and fast ships without interference. This alone required 255 minesweepers

As the flotilla approached the beaches it was to split up, portions would sweep the fire support channels inshore, others would sweep the boat lanes for the landing craft. The remainder would sweep lateral channels along the beaches, and then clear the large offshore assembly and anchorage areas. These phases were divided into over 100 discrete operations, each requireing timely and accurate completion.[85]

This operation had to be carried out without alerting the Germans, as minesweeping would be seen as a definite indicator of impending assault. This was accomplished by

---

[83] Elliot, 111.

[84] Samuel E. Morison, <u>History of United States Naval Operations in World War II</u>, 15 vols. (Boston: Little, Brown and Co., 1984) XI: 78.

[85] Elliot, 113.

sweeping at night when within sight of the French coast, and by delaying the start of the minesweeping until 4 June. As the minesweepers cleared the channels south from area Z the invasion force followed close behind, with the concept being that as dawn broke, the boat lanes and fire support areas would be cleared and the assault could begin.

Despite extensive German mining in mid-channel, of the over 4000 ships which made the crossing, only the American minesweeper USS Osprey was lost. The surprise of the assault was nearly lost when the minesweepers approached within eleven miles of the French coast on the day prior to the invasion. Admiral Ruge believes these units were observed but not reported.[86] Had they been, and had the Germans reacted, they could hardly have failed to notice the massive concentration of shipping then building in Area Z and the adjacent channels. Several of the minesweeping units were observed and engaged by German radar laid guns on the St. Marcouf Islands near Omaha Beach but no reaction other than gunfire occured.[87]

By 0500 the minesweepers were within two miles of the coast, and heavily engaged by shore batteries as they swept the final sections if the boat lanes. These were quickly cleared but many of the mines were equipped with actuation

---

[86] Ruge. 176.

[87] Elliot. 115.

delays and continued to claim victims for many days. The earlier sweeping of the fire support areas allowed the supporting bombardment ships to put a heavy counterbattery fire on the German guns. This allowed the sweepers the freedom to complete the final portions of their plan without excessive interference.[88] It also allowed for the 40 minute pre-assault preperatory fire mission.

The assault began at 0630, 6 June 1944, takeing the Germans by surprise. Among the many reasons why the Germans were surprised a large portion of the credit must be given to the minesweeping force. Sufficient numbers were assembled to allow the rapid sweeping of a large area to an acceptable confidence level. The minesweeping forces had the advantage of, in the British case, nearly five years of experience dealing with the threat and had become masters in the field.

This British experience had allowed the growth of a large body of professionals ,of sufficient rank, to plan and execute a complex and delicate minesweeping operation. Every minesweeping group attached to the amphibious task force was commanded by a Royal Navy officer.[89] Without this body of equipment and expertise the invasion of Normandy would not have been possible. Had the amount of equipment

---

[88] Elliot. 115.

[89] Morison. 335.

been halved, the clearance times would have been doubled for the same confidence factor, and the exposure and risk of German detection increased by a like amount. The area could theoretically have been swept in the same amount of time for half the confidence factor, but at increased risk of ship loss. As it was the casualties from mines in the naval forces exceeded all other causes.[90]

The surprise prevented the Germans from using one of their newest undersea weapons, the pressure mine, from disrupting the invasion. This mine, nicknamed the "oyster" used the pressure wave of a ship passing overhead to move a diaphragm and close a firing circuit. It was available in simple pressure, combined magnetic-pressure, and combined magnetic pressure variations. The Germans had begun production of these devices in 1943, but, fearing compromise, withheld them from operational use. They planned to employ them against the impending Allied invasion.[91] By May 1944 they had amassed over 2000 of these mines at the Le Mans airfield, with two squadrons of minelaying aircraft to emplace them.[92] Between 6 June and 31 July over 400 of these mines were laid in the invasion area, disrupting assault traffic seriously.

---

[90] Morison. 94.

[91] Elliot. 117.

[92] Elliot. 117.

Had this occured earlier the disruption would have been more severe, as these mines are virtually unsweepable. The only countermeasure is to slow shipping speed to the point that pressure waves are not generated by the hulls. The safe speeds in knots for Normandy were: [93]

DEPTH	5	10	15	20
BB	0	2.5	4	6
DD	3.5	7	11	14
APA	0	4	6	9

Figure Nine

As mentioned in the preface to this chapter, amphibious assaults are notoriously sensitive to disruptions of timing and synchronization. The effect of such an unplanned speed restriction would be to disrupt buildup of the beachhead, deny fire support, and delay the movement of logistics over the shore. Because of the initial surprise, the Germans were unable to employ these weapons until the initial assault phases were ended, and the disruption, while significant, was not critical. The final irony of this story is that the summer storms of 1944 which destroyed the artifical harbors caused such a heavy swell that they

---

[93] Elliot. 118. BB are battleships, DD are destroyers, APA are assault transports. Depths are in fathoms (6 feet per fathom).

actuated the pressure side of these mines. makeing them sweepable as plain acoustic or magnetic weapons.[94]

The British cleared 860 mines from their sector between June 6 and September 30, losing 14 ships in the process. The Americans cleared 454 in their sector for a loss of 34 ships, six of which were minesweepers.[95] Note the British rate of loss as compared to the American.

An examination of the Normandy operation in view of the subordinate thesis questions follows.

Q. Does the loss of tactical surprise make a large scale amphibious operation unfeasible.

A. In this case yes. The Germans had sufficient forces in the Normandy area to confine the assault forces on the beach. The surprise achieved did not allow them sufficient reaction time to mass combat power against the invasion force.

Q. Based on historical data, what level of losses can be expected by amphibious forces entering a mined area.

A. In this case 48 ships were lost for a total of 1354 mines swept, yielding a loss ratio of 1 ship per 28.2 mines cleared. Total losses were less than one percent of the invasion force.

---

[94] Elliot. 119.

[95] Lott. 289.

Q. What level of mine clearance effort is required to sweep an amphibious operating area for a large scale amphibious assault.

A. To sweep the amphibious operating area for Utah Beach, where one division landed across two beaches, required the services of 85 minesweepers for the 24 hours preceeding the assault. Further clearance and maintenance sweeping continued for three months.

Q. Given the above answer, and the assets available in 1991, what would be the duration of such a sweep effort.

A. There were 28 minecraft in commission in the U.S. Navy on 1 January 1991. Therefore, to conduct the assault sweeping portion alone operation in 1991 would require three days using every mine warfare vessel flying the U.S. flag.

Q. Given historical data, what level of losses can be expected by the mine clearance forces.

A. Seven minecraft were lost at Normandy. 2.28 percent of the total committed.

Q. Given the historical loss rates, and current force levels, would expected losses render an amphibious assault force combat ineffective.

A. The two MEB amphibious task force employed in Operation Desert Storm employed 31 ships. At the Normandy loss rate of one ship per 28.2 mines the force would have been eliminated.

Q. Are current minesweeping techniques adequate to clear an amphibious operating area in a timely manner.

A. The techniques used at Normandy differ only in small technical detail from those used today. The answer, therefore is yes, technique is adequate.

Normandy yields the following lessons concerning the mine and amphibious warfare relationship. First, there is no substitute for numbers. The 85 minesweepers used at Utah were needed to open that beach quickly. Even with the massive air and naval bombardment it was impossible to completely isolate the beachhead and every additional hour worked in the Germans favor.

Mine technology is important but not critical. The Germans were superb innovators who pushed mine warfare technology to where it is today. The British were equally adept at the technology of countermeasures. Even the introduction of the pressure mine failed to cause more than a temporary setback. Aggressive foreign material acquisition and exploitation programs allowed the Allies to stay one step ahead of the Germans throughout the process.

Experience and training are paramount. The complex 100 serial minesweeping operation could not have been carried out without the experienced officers and crews. These men swept the beach areas under heavy German fire without interruption. This stands in direct contrast to the events of Gallipoli.

WONSAN

As occurs after all wars, the naval forces of the United States and her Allies were rapidly drawn down after the Japanese surrender.

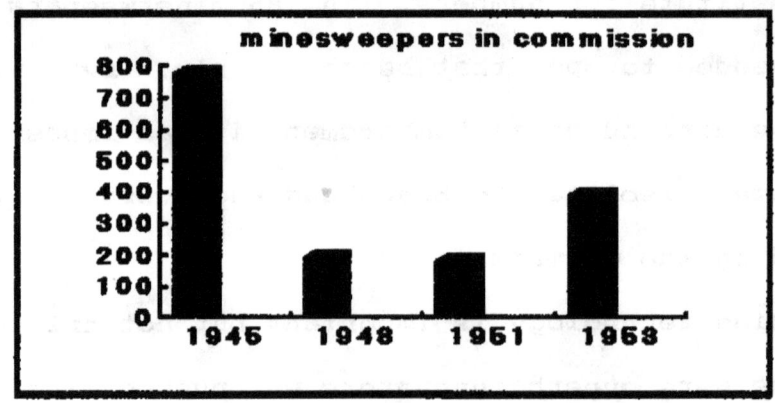

Figure Ten

The United States Pacific Fleet, lost 99 percent of its over 500 mine warfare ships, 3000 officers, and 30,000 enlisted men.[95] In the five years between 1945 and 1950 the ships were sold, mothballed, or scrapped and the crews discharged or dispersed. The primary task in the Pacific became the clearance of the vast numbers of mines the U.S. had laid in Japanese waters. This was essentially completed by February 1946, and the U.S. minesweeper fleet departed for home waters and demobilization. By May 1946, USS

---

[95] Lott. 269.

Waxwing was the sole remaining American minesweeper in the country.[96]

The demobilization of forces was matched by a lessening in official interest. At wars end the Pacific fleet mine warfare force was led by a flag officer with a large staff. This staff was charged with developing plans, ensuring the material readiness of the mine warfare force, and enforceing uniform standards of training. In January 1947, this command was disestablished and its responsibilities divided up amongst other major staffs. With this dissolution in focus, standards of training and readiness in the mine forces rapidly decreased.[97]

The Soviets had conducted extensive mining operations in World War II in the Baltic and Black Seas, and as mentioned in the introduction, had used mines early in the twentieth century against the Japanese at Port Authur. They had amassed large stockpiles of mines, and as an added bonus, had captured the German scientists and factories which were producing the advanced influence fuzed ground mines referred to in the Normandy study. They were in a unique position to assist the North Koreans in combatting a sea power.

---

[96] Lott, 265.

[97] United States Pacific Fleet, "Korean War: U.S. Pacific Fleet Operations, Interim Evaluation Report Number 1", Microfilm Roll DD, Combined Arms Research Library, Ft. Leavenworth, KS, 1091.

The Soviets conducted an analysis of the Korean coastline with an eye towards the most efficient use of mines. They correctly noted that the west, or Yellow Sea coast, is a mass of inlets, mudflats, and estuaries with a large tidal variation. It was thus not amenable to mining or amphibious operations. The east coast, bordered by the Sea of Japan, is the exact opposite. Due to the high eastern mountains most rivers in Korea drain to the west and the alluvial shallows found there are not present on the opposite shore. The coastline is straight, the water deep relatively close inshore, the currents and tidal range are small. It is therefore ideal for both amphibious and mine warfare.

Abetted by the Soviets, on June 25, 1950, the North Koreans invaded across the 38th parallel. They rapidly pushed the South Korean forces to the rear, and the U.S. government decided to reinforce the beleagured South Koreans with the 24th Infantry and First Cavalry Divisions. These units were administratively landed, thrown ill-prepared into battle, and defeated by the North Koreans. The Allied forces were inexorably forced into a pocket on the southern tip of the Korean peninsula, the "Pusan Perimeter". To lift this seige General Douglas Macarthur conducted Operation Chromite, the amphibious assault at Inchon.

Chromite was a large operation involving the landing of one Marine Division and involving over 200 ships. As such it was the equivalent of a Saipan, or one of the Normandy beaches. To support this task force the U.S. Navy could muster only Mine Squadron Three, consisting of seven ships under the command of Capt. Richard T. Spofford, USN.[98]

Due to the large tidal range Inchon was not amenable to mining. Moored contact mines set to strike ships at high tide were exposed at low tide and could be easily disposed of or marked and avoided. The one field laid at Inchon was thus discovered by destroyers Mansefield and DeHaven, and cleared by gunfire. The minesweeper squadron began sweeping at 0600, 15 September, found no mines, and was clear of the amphibious operation area by that afternoon.[99]

The tremendous success of the Inchon landing and it associated operations caused the collapse of North Korean organized resistance. The assault forces linked up with Allied forces advancing northward, recaptured Seoul, and began a northward pursuit of the rapidly withdrawing North Korean Peoples Army.

Recieving permission from the JCS on 9 October 1950 to cross the 38th parallel, General Macarthur (CINCUNC) directed his staff to prepare a plan to coordinate the main Eighth Army drive on Pyongyang with and amphibious assault on the east coast at Wonsan. This assault would advance

---

[98] Lott, 271.

[99] Lott, 271.

westward and link up with the Eighth Army at Pyongyang, thereby trapping the North Korean elements east and south of the Kaesong-Pyongyang corridor.[100] The plan was prepared and forwarded to the JCS on 28 September 1950, and approved three days later. D-Day was established as 20 October 1950.

Wonsan lies on the east coast of the Korean peninsula 80 miles north of the 38th parallel. It is in a large bay providing an excellent fleet anchorage with depths ranging from 10 fathoms to 15 feet over a hard sand bottom. Tides and currents are negligible. The beaches are of moderate gradient and good trafficability. There are good mobility corridors extending north, southwest and west. In short, it is an obviously excellent choice for an amphibious objective area.

Forces for this assault were to be the 1st Marine Division and the 7th Infantry Division, embarking at Inchon and Pusan respectivly.[101] Because of the requirement to embark such a large force using the barely adequate Korean facilities, the entire operation was time-constrained from the beginning, particularly given that the 1st MarDiv was engaged clearing the Uijongbu corridor when the order was issued.[102]

---

[100] Lynn Montross and Nicholas Canzona, <u>United States Marine Operations in Korea</u> 5 vols. (Washington, D.C.: Headquarters, United States Marine Corps, 1957) III: 9.

[101] Montross and Canzona. III: 11.

[102] Montross and Canzona. III: 13.

Admiral C. Turner Joy, CINCNAVFE, issued the initiating directive on 1 October to Vice Admiral Arthur D. Struble, COM JTF-7. This order prescribed the following missions for the amphibious task force:

1. To maintain a blockade of the Korean east coast.

2. To furnish air and naval gunfire support to the Eighth Army as required.

3. To conduct pre D-Day operations in the Wonsan area as required.

4. To load and transport X Corps to Wonsan, providing cover and support en route.

5. To seize by amphibious assault, occupy, and defend a beachhead in the Wonsan area on D-Day.

6. To provide air, naval gunfire, and initial logistical support to X Corps at Wonsan until relieved.

The document further warned:

> The strong probability exists that the ports and possible landing beaches under control of the North Koreans have been recently mined. The sighting of new mines floating in the area indicates that mines are being seeded along the coast.[103]

Events unfolded rapidly, by 2 October the 7th Infantry Division was enroute to Pusan and by 7 October the 1st Marine Division was at Inchon preparing to embark. The

---

[103] Montross and Canzona, III: 13.

necessary shipping having been assembled, the Marines began their embarkation on 8 October and the 7th Inf Div on the 9th. All units had sailed by 17 October.[104] The 122 ship task force was enroute to the objective.

Ironically, by the time the amphibious task force sailed the operation was no longer necessary. North Korean resistance had further deteriorated and their withdrawal had become a rout. The Republic of Korea (ROK) Army entered Wonsan on 10 October and secured the port the next day. At this point CINCUNC considered changing the objective but was dissuaded by his advisors. The decision was made to land the X Corps at Wonsan, in an administrative vice tactical operation.[105]

Task Group 95.6 began minesweeping on 10 October in preparation for the assault. This force, consisting of 12 American, 9 Japanese, and 3 Korean minesweepers, had been warned of the presence of mines. Helicopters from the cruiser USS Rochester had reported moored mines "too numerous to count". These mines were easily swept and by evening on 10 October a channel 3000 yards wide and 12 miles long had been cleared.[106]

---

[104] Montross and Canzona. III: 23.

[105] Montross and Canzona. III: 22.

[106] Lott. 275.

As the sweepers reached the thirty fathom line the USS Rochester's helicopter reported five additional lines of moored mines obstructing the passage to the beach. Attempting to save time, Captain Spofford began to utilize divers to mark mines, and, on the morning of 12 October, attempted a technique known as "brute force minesweeping". This involves using aerial bombs or depth charges in an attempt to clear paths through minefields, the theory being that the concussion will cause adjacent mines to detonate. It had been unsuccessful in World War II and it was unsuccessful in Korea.[107] The field was little effected.

The minefield had been laid by Koreans under the supervision of professional Soviet mine experts. Intelligence had reported the presence of thirty such Soviet personel in the Wonsan area between 16 July and 4 October. They had designed a field which provided the optimum defensive barrier and was interlocked with overwatching shore batteries.[108] Unbeknownst to the Americans, they had also planted delayed action magnetic mines in the field.

Mechanical minesweeping again began late in the morning of the 12th. Minesweepers USS Pledge, USS Pirate, and USS Incredible penetrated the minefield at 1112, shortly

---

[107] Lott, 275, and Montross and Canzona, III: 28.

[108] Harry M. Edwards, "A Naval Lesson of the Korean Conflict," *United States Naval Institute Proceedings*, 80 (Dec 1954) 1338.

afterward Pirate struck a mine and sank almost immediately. At 1220, USS Pledge suffered the same experience. The shore batteries handicapped the frantic efforts to rescue the crews of both ships.[109]

At this point a more conservative approach was adopted. Helicopters, flying boats, and divers were used to search for and mark mines which were then swept by the small wooden hulled minesweepers Mockingbird, Chatterer, Redhead, and Kite. Using this method a channel was cleared in five days, with the loss of one small Japanese minesweeper. The channels into Wonsan were to be declared cleared by 19 October, one day prior to the scheduled landing.[110]

On 19 October as Redbird and ROK YMS 516 conducted final check sweeps of the channel, the Korean minesweeper was blasted literally into splinters by a large explosion. The culprit was a Soviet M-KB magnetic mine with an 1800 lb high explosive warhead. These had been laid in the bay with 12 ship delay counter. The amphibious operating area was closed until these mines could be swept, a task not completed until October 25th.[111] Approximately 3000 mines had been laid, of which 255 were swept.

---

[109] Montross and Canzona. III: 29.

[110] Lott. 277.

[111] Lott. 277.

The 1st Marine Division began landing on the afternoon of the 25th. As they came ashore they were greeted by two sites, the first was a sign reading "This Beach Brought to You Courtesy of Mine Squadron Three", the other was the Bob Hope USO troupe setting up for a show. They had been delayed 5 days, in what the embarked troops derisively called "Operation Yo-Yo", so named for the ceaseless north-south steaming of the transport shipping.[112] No further large amphibious assaults were attempted during the Korean War.

The failure at Wonsan was tempered by the success of the ground forces so the actual tactical loss was insignificant. Nevertheless, it severly shocked a Navy which had grown accustomed to exercising complete control of the sea. The simple fact was that over 40,000 men were delayed offshore for five days, an event which could have proven fatal in differing circumstances. A similar occurance at Normandy would have been disasterous. It galvanized the Navy into building a fleet of over 150 non-magnetic minesweepers in the 1950's.[113] The remnants of that fleet served in the Persian Gulf in 1991.

An examination of the Wonsan landing in light of the subordinate thesis questions follows.

---

[112] Montross and Canonza, 30.

[113] Lott, 285.

Q. Does the loss of tactical surprise make a large-scale amphibious assault unfeasible.

A. In this case, no. The loss of surprise, while complete, was negated by the rapid advance of the Eighth Army and their securing of the landing force's objectives.

Q. Based on historical data, what level of losses can be expected by amphibious forces entering a mined area.

A. In this case four ships were lost for the 255 mines swept, a ratio of one ship per 64 mines lifted. These four ships were all minesweepers. The low casualty rate was due to the deliberate decision not to attempt to force the minefield.

Q. What level of mine clearance effort is required to sweep an amphibious operating area for a large scale amphibious assault.

A. The operation at Wonsan approximated the Utah beach portion of the Normandy landing in numbers of troops, beaches, and shipping. To clear such an area in 24 hours would require approximately 85 trained minesweepers, that number used at Normandy. The 35 available, with their marginal state of training, were insufficient for the task.

Q. Given the information above, and the forces available in 1991, what would be the duration of such a sweep effort.

A. The 28 minesweepers currently in the force would require approximately 6.5 days to conduct this operation.

Q. Would the sweep effort alert the enemy to potential landing areas.

A. In this case, the enemy had already determined the most likely landing areas by conducting a close hydrographic analysis of his coastline. The sweep effort did provide confirmation, and the forces were engaged by enemy shore batteries until the town was cleared from landward.

Q. Given historical data, what level of losses can be expected by the mine clearance forces.

A. At Wonsan, all losses were to minesweepers. Of the thirty-five employed, four were sunk for a percentage loss of 11.5%. This loss equates to 3.2% of the total force.

Q. Given the information developed above, and current force levels, would losses render an amphibious assault force combat ineffective.

A. In this case no. No measure of the experienced versus the expected losses yield a potential loss of more than 12 %. In an eighteen ship MEB amphibious task force this would equate to a loss of two ships. The delay at Wonsan was more telling than the actual or potential losses.

Q. Are current minesweeping techniques adequate to clear an amphibious operating area in a timely manner.

A. In this case, yes. The benign environment experienced after 12 October would have allowed the use of airborne mine countermeasures and clearance diving teams. Without interference, these can synchronize their efforts with surface mine countermeasures forces and achieve rapid results.

Q. How does mine technology affect the duration of minesweeping operations.

A. In this case the effort was extended an additional five days by the discovery of the KB-Krab magnetic mines.

As potentially disasterous as it was. Wonsan did provide the Navy with an opportunity to exercise some new capabilities and a plethora of lessons learned or relearned. A new innovation was the use of helicopters and patrol aircraft to locate minefields. The coordination of these with the underwater demolition teams and surface minesweepers directly contributed to the low casualty rate.

Intelligence is paramount. The UN forces were aware of the Soviet involvement in North Korean mine warfare. They were not aware that over 4000 mines. many of the latest type. had been shipped to North Korea and were being laid undet the supervision of experts. At Wonsan. information obtained from local civilians enabled the naval mine experts to identify the types of mines laid and their approximate locations. This greatly enhanced the speed of the clearance operation.

There is no substitute for numbers. The U.S. Pacific Fleet began the Korean war with 19 minecraft, down from over 1.000 five years previously. There were no small boat minesweepers and consequently no capability to sweep mines in water less than six feet deep. There was a commensurate lack of experienced personnel and equipment of all types. The effort would have suffered more were it not for the participation of the Japanese and ROK sweep units.

The real lesson of Wonsan was that the mine had not lost its usefullness, despite the primacy of the aircraft carrier and the jet aircraft in naval warfare. The Navy learned from this incident that the powerful amphibious forces are completely ineffective if they can't get ashore. Unwilling to sacrifice the amphibious option, the USN embarked on an ambitious program which was to add over 150 minecraft to the fleet by 1960.

DESERT SHIELD/DESERT STORM

The fleet of wooden minesweepers dwindled slowly through the 1960's and 70's. The advent of the nuclear submarine, the nuclear powered aircraft carrier, and the guided missile diverted attention from the dirty and mundane task of minesweeping. The development of airborne minesweeping using the CH-53 helicopter promised to eliminate the need for the aging surface minesweeping force. As age and indifference took its toll, the force began to slowly shrink. The minesweeping conducted in Haiphong after the cease fire was conducted exclusively by helicopters, as was the clearance of the Suez Canal after 1973.

Lacking resources, removed from the mainstream, and rarely operational, the minesweepers languished at Charleston, S.C., and Tacoma, WA. The force did not receive top flight personnel as the main stream navy focused elsewhere. The minesweeper became regarded chiefly as an early command opportunity, one to be completed and then left as rapidly as possible. In 1968 the Navy had 65 ocean going minesweepers, 24 coastal minesweepers, and two mine countermeasures ships designed to carry small minesweeping launches and helicopters into an assault.[114] By 1991 this force had shrunk to 28 total.

A portion of this depletion was due to commonly agreed military strategy in NATO. The U.S. Navy viewed the Soviet Union as its primary enemy and carried the brunt of the strike power projection mission. The mine countermeasures problem was left to the Europeans, in whose waters the majority of these operations would undoubtedly take place. Commanders like NATO's Commander in Chief Channel (CINCCHAN) formed multi-national minesweeping forces and assumed the role of mine warfare proponent. As a result of this policy, the European members of NATO forged ahead in the development of mine warfare tactics and technology. The Germans pioneered the Troika system of remote control minesweeping craft, and the Italian shipbuilding industry perfected the use of glass reinforced plastic (GRP) as a substitute for wood. The latest American minesweeper, USS Avenger (MCM 1), commissioned in 1988, was of wooden construction. American experiments in the use of GRP ended with the aborted Cardinal class minesweeper-hunter.

The 1980's saw two incidents which required the deployment and employment of American mine warfare forces. The first occurred in 1985, when the Libyan Ro-Ro Ghat deposited a number of mines in the approaches to the Saudi

---

[114] Norman Polmar, *United States Naval Institute Proceedings*, 105(February 1979): 117-119.

port of Jeddah. These were advanced bottom mines, with dual acoustic/magnetic fusing. The first indication of their presence was the damaging of a number of merchant vessels as the neared the port. At the request of the Saudi government, American and British mine countermeasures forces deployed to Jeddah and began to sweep. The U.S. contingent, consisting of USS Shreveport and a detachment of minesweeping helicopters, swept the harbor without results. The British recovered one mine which was exploited for intelligence information.

The Iran-Iraq war, which began in September 1980, had already featured significant amounts of mine warfare. Both belligerents had received mine stocks from their benefactors and both attempted to use them. Neither side met with much success in their initial efforts. The Iraqi's attempted to mine the Iranian ports in the Northern Persian Gulf, and succeeded in damaging a number of merchant ships, none critically.

The Iranians conducted similar operations against the Iraqi ports of Umm Qasr and Basrah with similar results. Neither side had conducted the necessary intelligence analysis to determine where the mines would be most effective. Additionally, they made technical errors in deploying the mines and so reduced their effectiveness.

Both sides rapidly withdrew from offensive mining, and limited their efforts to laying defensive fields around their own coastal facilities. Both the Iraqis and the Iranians laid extensive defensive fields in the northern Persian Gulf, primarily around Kharg Island and the Iraqi offshore terminals at Mina al Bakr and Khor Amaya.

The war escalated in mid 1984 with the advent of what became known as the "Tanker War". This featured aircraft from both sides attacking merchant shipping bound for each others ports. The Iranians rapidly added a new twist as their navy began attacking shipping throughout the Persian Gulf.

The continued Iranian depredations led Kuwait, with the support of the Gulf Cooperation Council nations, to appeal for assistance in ensuring access to its oil outloading ports. This was accomplished through the subterfuge of placing the Kuwaiti Oil Tanker Company vessels under American, British, and Soviet flags. This entitled the ships to the protection of the warships flying their flags. This operation was code named "Earnest Will".

The Iranians , unable to combat the sophisticated warships of the major powers, struck back with mining. The first Earnest Will convoy made history when one of the reflagged tankers, SS Bridgeton, struck a mine near Farsi Island. This galvanized the U.S. and other nations into a response and a minesweeping fleet was dispatched. The USS Guadalcanal was pulled from her participation in exercise

Bright Star, routed to Diego Garcia to pick up minesweeping helicopters and leave her marines, and sent to the Gulf.

Three U.S. minesweepers were sent from each coast. Due to the age of the ships and a requirement to minimize operation hours on their non-magnetic diesel engines, the ships were towed to the Persian Gulf. Once their the units integrated and began regular sweeping of the shipping lanes.

Ships continued to strike mines, as the Iranians reseeded fields which had been swept. This abated somewhat in late 1987 with the capture and subsequent destruction of the minelayer Iran Ajr, and ceased entirely after the April 1988 engagements with the U.S. Navy which followed the mining of the USS Samuel B. Roberts. Following the cessation of hostilities in September 1988, a multi-national force swept the Gulf, completing the operation in the spring of 1990.

Following the invasion of Kuwait, an 18 ship amphibious task force sailed from Norfolk on 15 August. Embarked was the 4th Marine Expeditionary Brigade under the command of Major General Harry Jenkins. The amphibious task force was commanded by Rear Admiral John B. Laplante. The mine countermeasures forces departed several days later on board a Dutch heavy lift ship. Upon arriving in theater the amphibious task force assumed station in the North Arabian Sea and the mine countermeasures force established a base in Abu Dhabi at the port of Mina Rashid.

After a lengthy trip essentially in dry-dock, the mine force ships required machinery realignments before becoming operational. A degaussing facility was also established to aid in reducing the magnetic signatures of the units. An ad-hoc task force, Commander U.S. Mine Countermeasures Group was established to oversee these activities.

In November 1990 units of the amphibious task force conducted an exercise amphibious assault on the Saudi coastline north of Jubail. The site was approximately 70 miles south of the Kuwait-Saudi border. The event was heavily publicized, in a move designed to foster Iraqi concerns over the U.S. amphibious capability. The exercise was abbreviated due to heavy weather exceeding the safe operating limits of the landing craft involved.

The exercise had a profound effect on the Iraqis. Several weeks after the conclusion of Imminent Thunder, the first floating mines began to appear in the vicinity of the Saudi oil field of Saffiniyeh. These mines were free of sea growth, indicating they had been recently laid, and of a design never before encountered. They were designated LUGM-145, after the Arabic acronym for mine, the 145 was the weight of the explosive charge in kilograms. The heavy weather had caused the Iraqi mines to part their moorings and float south on the prevailing current.

The mines began to be found in ever increasing numbers throughout December. There are no effective countermeasures for floating mines other than an alert lookout and a good explosive ordnance disposal team. The mines claimed no victims, and their discovery and destruction became quite routine for the units involved.

The location of the minefields in the northern Persian Gulf was a mystery. Friendly ships and aircraft were prohibited from operating north of a line extending east from the Kuwait-Saudi border so surveillance was impossible. Through the analysis of hydrographic conditions some areas were determined to be more likely to contain mines. This method of analysis would prove flawed.

When the war began on 16 January coalition naval forces quickly wrested control of the northern Persian Gulf from the Iraqi's. By 31 January 1991, the two T-43 minesweepers and the Spasilac-class salvage tug, the primary culprits, had been either sunk of extensively damaged.[115] Naval units, particularly USS Curts and USS Nicholas, began to operate in the area. They sighted and destroyed many mines but encountered no minefields.

As the preparations for the ground war began, it became obvious that the Joint Forces Command-East, and the USMC forces driving north would require naval gunfire support. To provide this a properly aligned channel would have to be swept to allow the 16 in guns of Missouri and Wisconsin

---

[115] Norman Friedman, *Desert Victory-The War for Kuwait*, (Annapolis: Naval Institute Press, 1991), 363.

access to their targets. Aboard the amphibious task force, oblivious to their deception role, it had become apparent that mine countermeasures support would be needed if a landing were to be conducted. The ATF had grown to 31 ships by this point and required considerable sea room. The large deck air capable ships alone required 175 square miles of clear water. Additionally, boat lanes ,assembly areas, and fire support areas would have to be swept.

At this point there were but 14 ships and one helicopter squadron available for this task, of that 14 only the four U.S. and three British sweepers were committed to wartime sweeping. With these forces it was estimated that two to three weeks would be required to complete the minesweeping to a confidence level of 70%.

The mine sweeping was begun in mid February 1991 under the control of Commander, U.S. MCM Group embarked in USS Tripoli. The minesweepers had not discovered a single mine when, at 0430 18 February, the Tripoli struck a moored contact mine of the LUGM-145 variety. This mine opened a 16 by 20 foot hole in the hull, flooded three compartments, and caused the ship to temporarily lose power.[116] She remained in the area for two days until worsening weather caused the commander to order her withdrawn. At 0716 the USS Princeton, providing anti air coverage 10 miles distant, was

---

[116] J.M. Martin, "We Still Haven't Learned", United States Naval Institute Proceedings, 117(July 1991): 64.

shaken by a large explosion near the stern. She had actuated an influence mine, probably of the Misar Manta variety. The stern was buckled upward by the explosion, forcing the port propeller shaft out of alignment. She crept from the minefield on her starboard shaft and was towed to Bahrain for repairs.

The minesweepers found themselves on the fringes of two large minefields which blocked access to the Kuwaiti coastline. They began sweeping mines in earnest and by 25 February had cleared a 1000 yard channel through these mines to allow the battleships access to their firing positions.

Any possibility of an amphibious assault died with the mine detonations on the morning of 18 February. Had the employment of the afloat marines become necessary the minefields could have been swept more quickly, albeit to a lesser degree of confidence. Estimated casualties from mines alone for such an operation range from 3000-5000.[117] The Iraqis had planned for a mine density of 60 per nautical mile for depths between 10-40 feet, 800-1600 per nautical mile between the 10 ft curve and the beach, and 3200-6400 per nautical mile on the beach itself. The density between the 10 ft and 40 ft curves was achieved.[116] This equates to one mine approximately every 100 feet.

---

[117] Tom Phillpott and David Steigman, Navy Times, 47(September 2, 1991), 12

[116] Friedman, 211.

This level of density, particularly with the larger influence fused ground mines, is essentially impenetrable. The magnetic disturbance of a large ship extends well beyond that distance and the larger amphibious assault ships are only exceeded in size by aircraft carriers. By pulsing the magnetic sweeping equipment at very high amperages, the minesweepers can detonate the mines outside the danger radius. Despite this assurance it is still a tedious and dangerous process.

Shortly after the cease fire the Iraqi government turned over charts depicting the areas mined. They had emplaced slightly over 1600 mines of various types in a belt extending from the Kuwait-Saudi border to the Al Faw peninsula. This established a cordon which isolated the Kuwaiti coast from any naval action.

With the locations of the mines known, and the threat of hostilities gone, the minesweepers were able to proceed apace. Several European and Asian countries which had withheld their forces during hostilities now released them, and the minesweeping force grew to 25. Of this number two German units were of the latest and most advanced variety, employing the Troika remote control minesweeping system.

Fortunately for the minesweepers, a large number of the Iraqi mines were maldeployed and failed to function correctly.[117] Even with this boon, and the increase in the force, the Persian Gulf was not declared mine free until mid September 1992, over six months after wars end. Despite their low lethality, they accomplished what the Iraqis desired. They kept the marines from attacking their shores.

Had an amphibious assault been required, the breaching of the Iraqi minefield would have been of such duration and level of effort as to render surprise out of the question. The loss of surprise in the small land area of Kuwait, with an Iraqi armor division in reserve less than 10 miles from the proposed landing beaches at Al Ahmadi, would likely have been fatal.

The truly discouraging feature of the Desert Storm mine warfare episode is our failure to heed the lessons we had just learned in Earnest Will. We knew that the Persian Gulf was particularly amenable to mining, and we knew the Iraqis had accumulated experience in mine warfare over their ten year conflict with the Iranians. Nevertheless, we stumbled blindly into their minefields just as we had 41 years previously at Wonsan. The magnitude of this particular failure was eclipsed by the magnificence of the victory.

An examination of this operation in light of the subordinate thesis questions follows.

---

[117]. James Clark, Interview by author, 10 March 1992, Ft. Leavenworth, KS.

Q. Does the loss of tactical surprise make a large scale amphibious assault unfeasible.

A. In this case no. The problem was rendered moot by the decision to use amphibious forces as a deception and by the rapid victory by the ground forces.

Q. Based on historical data, what level of losses can be expected by amphibious forces entering a mined area.

A. Three ships were damaged while sweeping 1600 mines, yielding one ship for every 533 mines lifted. For this operation the data is less valid due to foreknowledge of mine locations and the demonstrated Iraqi ineptitude. The stated figure of 3000-5000 would equate to the loss of 6-10 ships, or 19%-32% of the total force.

Q. What level of mine clearance effort is required to sweep an amphibious operating area for a large scale amphibious assault.

A. Given the seven ships available the figure quoted was two to three weeks. The relationship is linear, so given 14 ships of similar capability, the time would be one to one and one half. To achieve clearance in twenty four hours 56 minesweepers would have been required, exactly twice the total in the entire Navy inventory in 1991.

Q. Given the above information, and the assets available in 1991, what would be the duration of such a sweep effort.

A. Four to six days would have been required.

Q. Would the sweep effort alert an enemy to potential landing areas.

A. Given the situation at Gallipoli, Normandy, and Wonsan, a four to six day sweep effort would almost certainly alert the enemy to the landing area.

Q. Given historical data, what level of losses can be expected by the mine clearance forces.

A. In this case only one minesweeper, USS Leader, was damaged by a mine explosion of the 25 ships involved in clearance. This equates to a loss rate of 4%. This is attributable to the great degree of care taken by the clearance forces once the environment became essentially benign. The forces concentrated on locating and destroying individual mines vice sweeping and causing large numbers to detonate.

Q. Given the information developed above, would expected losses render an amphibious assault force combat ineffective.

A. In this case yes. The postulated 3000-5000 man or 6-10 ship loss would have been sufficient to stop the assault or radically alter its nature.

Q. Are current minesweeping techniques adequate to clear an amphibious operating area in a timely manner.

A. Yes. Current technique was adequate. This operation revealed a predilection for mine hunting and neutralization, a procedure which is far more time consuming, albeit safer.

Q. How does mine technology affect the duration of mine sweeping operations.

A. In this case the mix of high and low, Soviet and western technology in the mine fields lengthened the process. Each type of mine required specific sweep techniques and equipment. This necessitated a changeover every time differing types were encountered.

Q. Is the potential loss of the large scale amphibious assault a matter of great concern in the current strategic environment.

A. In this case, the loss was not felt since the amphibious operation was a deception.

As previously stated, the mine and amphibious warfare failures in Desert Storm were eclipsed by the successes of strike warfare. After some initial consternation, mine warfare is once again slipping towards oblivion. Of the six US mine countermeasures ships, four were over thirty five years old and will soon be decommissioned. The current surface force MCM plan calls for a force of 14 Avenger class mine countermeasures ships, and 20 Osprey class coastal mine hunters. Of these 20 mine hunters, only eight will be deployable. None will be capable of sweeping mines in their current configuration but will rely on mine detection and neutralization. This is the same timely process that took six months to clear the Persian Gulf.[119]

---

[119] James R. Guisti, "Surface Navy: The '90s and Beyond", *Surface Warfare,* 17(Jan/Feb 1992): 7.

CHAPTER FIVE

CONCLUSIONS AND RECOMMENDATIONS

To develop the conclusions it is necessary to return to chapter one and the original thesis question:

Has the proliferation of high technology sea mines eliminated tactical surprise in large scale amphibious assaults?

For Gallipoli the answer is yes. The mines employed there were high technology by the standard of the day. Their use by the Turks caused the British to expend considerable effort towards effecting their removal, and by this effort they alerted the commander that some event was impending. In this case they also prevented the Allies from fully supporting their landing forces and prevented the battle from being bought to a culmination.

In the case of Normandy the answer is no. The mines employed there were absolutely state of the art and included some types never before encountered. While inflicting damage they did not delay the assault, and their effect, while substantial, was not critical. The large and well seasoned mine countermeasures force was able to clear the mine fields with such alacrity that the Germans failed to notice their activities.

At Wonsan, the answer is a definite yes. The discovery of the MK-B mines lengthened the sweeping effort by a critical five days, the initial sweeping effort had taken eight days. A portion of this sweeping was conducted under the fire of North Korean shore batteries, a sure indication that surprise was lost.

In the case of Operation Desert Saber, as the amphibious assault would have been known, no exact answer is possible. To further the object of the deception a great deal of information about amphibious presence and the implied intent was fed to the Iraqis. Had an operation been required it would have been extremely difficult to conceal two-three weeks of minesweeping activity off an enemy coast. Modern surveillance and intelligence collection systems, which Iraq had in abundance, could easily detect this level of activity.

An examination of each case by subordinate thesis question shows the following:

Q. Does the loss of tactical surprise make a large scale amphibious operation unfeasible.

In the cases of Gallipoli and Normandy the answer is yes. In the case of Wonsan and Desert Storm surprise was not a factor.

Q. Based on historical data, what level of losses can be expected by amphibious forces entering a mined area.

The average loss rate was two percent in the three operations which involved combat.

Q. What level of effort is required to sweep an amphibious operating area for a large scale amphibious assault.

The answer depends on the level of threat and the degree of clearance confidence desired by the commander. As shown, to sweep a two MEB amphibious operating area in 24 hours to a confidence of 70% against a sophisticated threat requires 56 minesweepers. Wonsan was swept in 15 days by 35 minesweepers to a similar high level of confidence. Normandy was swept in 24 hours by over 300 ships, albeit to a lower level of confidence as shown by the higher loss rate.

Q. Given the above, and assets available in 1991, what would be the duration of such a sweep effort.

Given 1991 assets, Gallipoli could be swept in less than 24 hours, the entire Normandy operation could not be done by US assets alone in less than 12 days. Wonsan would require approximately six days, and the Persian Gulf in two to three days. This implies the commitment of all available resources.

Q. Would the sweep effort alert the enemy to potential landing areas.

In Gallipoli, Normandy, and Wonsan, yes. No exact answer is possible in the case of Desert Storm. Given the expected duration of the effort and the capabilities of the Iraqi surveillance systems, the most probable answer is yes.

Q. Given historical data, what level of losses can be expected by the mine clearance forces.

At Gallipoli 88.5%, at Normandy 11.5%, at Wonsan 2.28%, and 4% in the Persian Gulf. Wonsan and the Persian Gulf were both conducted free of interference from hostile action. Further research would be required to expand the sample size before a conclusion could be derived.

Q. Given the above data, would expected losses render an amphibious assault force combat ineffective.

Based on experienced loss in these operations the answer is no. I was unable to establish the derivation of the 3000-5000 figure quoted in the Persian Gulf study, however, it appears that these are based on no sweeping. Losses at Gallipoli, Normandy, or Wonsan rates would not render a modern amphibious task force combat ineffective.

Q. Are current minesweeping techniques adequate to clear an amphibious operating area in a timely manner.

In all four cases there was no problem with basic technique. The problems, where they appeared, were due to levels of training and availability of forces.

Q. How does mine technology affect the duration of minesweeping operations.

At Gallipoli, mine technology was not a factor. At Normandy, Wonsan, and in the Persian Gulf the higher technology mines encountered lengthened minesweeping times.

Q. Is the potential loss of the large scale amphibious assault a matter of great concern in the current strategic environment.

In Gallipoli and Normandy the answer is yes. The failure at Gallipoli lengthened the battle on the western front and hastened the downfall of the Russian government. A failure at Normandy would have had incalculable consequences. Wonsan was overcome by events, and the issue is moot regarding Desert Storm.

The main conclusions are:

1. Basic minesweeping tactics, techniques and procedures are adequate for today's threat.

2. Modern high-technology sea mines require a lengthy period to sweep.

3. Clearance times can be reduced by assigning more forces.

4. The U.S. mine countermeasures force is inadequate in numbers to perform a large scale assault sweep rapidly.

5. As the time spent minesweeping increases, the probability of achieving surprise decreases.

6. If a beachhead cannot be isolated, and surprise is not achieved, then an amphibious operation will probably fail.

In summary, the proliferation of high technology sea mines has reduced but not eliminated the achievement of surprise in the amphibious assault. The level of mine technology does not appear to be the determinant. Rather, the central issue seems to lie in two areas: force composition and size, and the level of training in the mine force.

I would recommend that further study be undertaken to design a mine countermeasures force capable of clearing a two MEB sized amphibious operating area to a high degree of confidence in 24 hours or less. Concurrent studies should be conducted to evaluate standards of readiness and training within the mine force, with an eye towards designing a system which would ensure these ships were always fully deployable and employable.

EVERY SHIP IS A MINESWEEPER—ONCE!

Appendix

U.S. Navy Ships, excluding Minecraft, sunk in World War II

Date	Name, Type, Tonnage	Location
1942		
April 26	USS Sturvesant, Destroyer, 1190	Key West, Florida
August 4	USS Tucker, Destroyer, 1500	Espiritu Santo
1943		
May 30	LCT-28, Landing Craft, 112	Mediterranean
June 4	PC-496, Sub Chaser, 261	Portugal
June 28	USS Redwing, Salvage, 950	Mediterranean
1944		
Jan. 26	LCI-32, Landing Craft, 175	Anzio
Feb. 18	YT-198, Tug, 70	Anzio

Date	Ship	Location
June 6	USS Corry, destroyer, 1630	Normandy
June 6	LCT-25, Landing Craft, 112	Normandy
June 6	LCT-30, Landing Craft, 112	Normandy
June 6	LCT-197, Landing Craft, 112	Normandy
June 6	LCT-294, Landing Craft, 112	Normandy
June 6	LCT-305, Landing Craft, 112	Normandy
June 6	LCT-332, Landing Craft, 112	Normandy
June 6	LCT-362, Landing Craft, 112	Normandy
June 6	LCT-555, Landing Craft, 134	Normandy
June 6	LCT-593, Landing Craft, 134	Normandy
June 6	LCT-597, Landing Craft, 134	Normandy
June 6	LCT-703, Landing Craft, 134	Normandy
June 6	LCT-777, Landing Craft, 134	Normandy

Date	Ship	Location
June 6	LCI-85, Landing Craft, 175	Normandy
June 6	LCI-91, Landing Craft, 175	Normandy
June 6	LCI_92, Landing Craft, 175	Normandy
June 6	LCI-232, Landing Craft, 175	Normandy
June 6	LCI-497, Landing Craft, 175	Normandy
June 7	LCT-458, Landing Craft, 112	Normandy
June 7	LCT-486, Landing Craft, 112	Normandy
June 7	USS Susan B. Anthony, Transport, 9352	Normandy
June 8	USS Glennon, Destroyer, 1630	Normandy
June 8	USS Meredith, Destroyer, 2200	Normandy
June 8	USS Rich, Destroyer, 1400	Normandy
June 8	LST-499, Landing Ship, 1490	Normandy

Date	Ship	Location
June 9	LCI-416, Landing Craft, 175	Normandy
June 11	LST-496, Landing Ship, 1490	Normandy
June 19	LST-423, Landing Ship, 1490	Normandy
Aug. 16	PT-202, Patrol Boat, 33	Southern France
Aug. 16	PT-218, Patrol Boat, 33	Southern France
Aug. 23	PT-555, Patrol Boat, 33	Mediterranean
Sept. 19	LCI-459, Landing Craft, 175	Palau
Oct 4	LCT-579, Landing Craft, 134	Palau
Nov. 18	LST-6, Landing Ship, 1490	Seine River

1945

Date	Ship	Location
Mar 26	USS Haligan, destroyer, 2050	Okinawa
Apr 8	PGM-18, motor gunboat, 85	Okinawa

Bibliography

Books

Elliot, Peter. *Allied Minesweeping in World War II*. (Annapolis: Naval Institute Press, 1979)

Friedman, Norman. *Desert Victory, The War for Kuwait*. (Annapolis, Naval Institute Press, 1991).

Hamilton, Sir Ian. *Gallipoli Diary*. (New York: George Doran and Co., 1920)

Hastings, Max. *The Korean War*. (New York: Simon and Shuster, 1987)

Head, C.O.. *A Glance at Gallipoli*. (London: Eyre and Spottiswoode, 1931)

Higgins, Trumbull. *Winston Churchill and the Dardanelles*. (Westport: Greenwood Press, 1963)

James, Robert Rhodes. *Gallipoli*. (New York: Macmillian, 1965)

Lott, Arnold. *Most Dangerous Sea*. (Annapolis: Naval Institute Press, 1959)

Mansefield, John. *Gallipoli*. (New York: Macmillian, 1917)

Moorehead, Alan. *Gallipoli*. (New York: Harper and Row, 1956)

Morison, Samuel Elliot. *History of United States Naval Operations in World War II*. (Boston: Little, Brown and Co. 1957) XI.

Nevinson, Henry W.. *The Dardanelles Campaign*. (New York: Henry Holt and Co., 1919)

Ruge, Friedrich. *Rommel in Normandy*.. (San Rafael: Presidio Press, 1979).

Sanders, Liman Von. *Five Years in Turkey*. (Baltimore: Williams and Wilkins, 1928)

Tuchman, Barbara. *The Guns of August*. (New York: Macmillian, 1962)

Articles

Ashbrook, A.W. "Naval Mines." <u>United States Naval Institute Proceedings</u>, 49 (Feb 1923): 303-312.

Bagby, Oliver. "Naval Mining and Naval MInes." <u>United States Naval Institute Proceedings</u>, 51 (Dec 1925): 2244-2257.

Baker, H. George, "The MSB Story: Little Ships Sweep the Sea to Keep It Free." <u>All Hands</u> 481 (February 1957): 2-5.

Baker, H. George, "The Mine Force: Wooden Ships and Iron Men." <u>All Hands</u> 481 (February 1957): 6-9.

Barker, E.L. "The Helicopter in Combat." <u>United States Naval Institute Proceedings</u>, 77 (Nov 1951): 1209.

Bellow, Steve. " In Search of the Killer Mine: Keeping Abreast of Minesweeping Technology." <u>All Hands</u>, 766 (November 1980): 14-19.

Berry, F. Clinton, "U.S. Navy Mine Warfare: Small But Not Forgotten." <u>Armed Forces Journal International</u> 128 (October 1979): 38-39.

Benz, Klaus. "Mine Warfare at Sea." <u>Armada International</u>, 14 (Dec/Jan 1990/91): 28-34.

Blouin, J.R., "Naval Mines and Modern Warfare." <u>National Defense</u> 60 (July-August 1975): 39-42.

Burke, Kip. "MCM's Master Mines". <u>Surface Warfare</u>, 17 (Jan/Feb 1992): 10-13.

Carter, Donald. "Mines-An Amphibious Threat." <u>Marine Corps Gazette</u> 32 (Dec 1948): 40-43.

Chriastiansen, Cyrus R., "A Minesweeping Shrimp Boat? A What?" <u>United States Naval Institute Proceedings</u> 107 (July 1981): 109-111.

Coletta, Paolo. "Mine Countermeasures." <u>United States Naval Institute Proceedings</u> 85 (Nov 1959): 82-96.

Cowie, J.S., "The Role of the U.S. Navy in Mine Warfare." <u>United States Naval Institute Proceedings</u> 91 (May 1965): 32-63.

Edwards, Harry. "A Naval Lesson of the Korean Conflict." United States Naval Institute Proceedings, 80(Dec 1954): 1337-1340.

Ennis, John. "Deep, Cheap, and Deadly Mine Warfare: The Most Economical Weapon-and the Most Neglected." Sea Power 17 (December 1974): 26-30.

Fang, Shi Wu. United States Naval Institute Proceedings, 67 (Jul 1941): 998.

Friedman, Norman. "U.S. MCM Programs." International Defense Review, 17 (Sept 1984): 1259-1268.

Friedman, Norman. "The Seaward Flank." United States Naval Institute Proceedings, 117 (Jul 1991): 81-83.

Frost, Roger. "Italy's Mine Makers." International Defense Review 17 (May 1986): 555-560.

Geisenheyner, Stefan. "Some Observations on Mine Warfare." Asian Defence Journal 4 (July-August 1980): 72-74.

Hewish, Mark. "Protecting Coastal Waters." 19 (Jan 1988): 29-32

Holbitzell, James J., "The Lessons of Mine Warfare." United States Naval Institute Proceedings 88 (December 1962): 32-37.

Hull, E.W. Seabrook. "Asleep in the Deep." Ordnance, 49 (September-October 1964): 158-161.

Kyle, Deborah M., "Mine Warfare." Armed Forces Journal International 119 (April 1982): 70-72.

Marriot, John. "A Survey of Modern Mine Warfare." Armada International, 11 (Sep/Oct 1987): 38-50.

Martin, J.M. "We Still Haven't Learned." United States Naval Institute Proceedings, 117 (Jul 1991): 64-68.

McCauley, Brian. "Operation End Sweep." United States Naval Institute Proceedings, 100 (Mar 1974): 19-25

Mcdonald, Wesley. "Mine Warfare: A Pillar of Maritime Strategy." United States Naval Institute Proceedings, 111 (Oct 1985): 53.

Miles, Sherman. "Notes on the Dardanelles Campaign of 1915", The Coastal Artillery Journal, undated.

Ostander, Colin. "Chaos at Shimonoseki." *United States Naval Institute Proceedings.* 73 (Jun 1947): 655.

Polmar, Norman. *Naval Institute Proceedings.* 105 (Feb 1979): 117-119.

Rairden, P.W. "The Importance of Mine Warfare." *United States Naval Institute Proceedings.* 78 (Aug 1952): 848.

Rogers, Edward. "Mines Wait, We Can't." *United States Naval Institute Proceedings.* 107 (Aug 1982): 57-63

Smith, R.H. *United States Naval Institute Proceedings.* 106 (Apr 1980): 29.

Stuart, Arthur. "The Beach Minefield." *Marine Corps Gazette.* 34 (Oct 1950): 58-65

Truver, Scott. "Tomorrows Fleet." *United States Naval Institute Proceedings.* 117 (Jul 1991): 52.

Van Nostrand, A.D. "Minesweping." *United States Naval Institute Proceedings.* 72 (Apr 1946): 505-509.

Wages, C.J. "Mines...Weapons That Wait." *United States Naval Institute Proceedings* 88 (May 1962): 103.

Walters, Brian. "Mines-A Neglected Aspect of Underwater Warfare." *Asian Defense Journal,* (June 1987): 77.

Wile, Ted. "Their Mine Warfare Capability." *United States Naval Institute Proceedings.* 107 (Oct 1982): 146-151.

Witt, Mike. "Countering the Sea Mine" *Asian Defense Journal.* (Oct 1988): 66-80.

Government Publications

Commander in Chief, U.S. Pacific Fleet. *Korean War Interim Evaluation Reports 1950-1953.* Honolulu, HI: Department of the Navy.

Ellis A. Johnson and David A. Katcher, *Mines Against Japan,* Silver Spring, MD. Naval Ordnance Laboratory, Department of the Navy, 1973.

Joint Chiefs of Staff. *JCS Pub 1, Dictionary of Military Terms*. Washington, DC: Department of Defense, 1990.

Joint Chiefs of Staff. *JCS Pub 3-02, Doctrine for Amphibious Operations*. Washington, DC: Department of Defense, 1986.

"Minecraft 1917-1969." In *Dictionary of American Naval Fighting Ships*. V. Washington, D.C.: Government Printing Office, 1970.

US Navy. *NWP 27-2, Mine Countermeasures*. Washington, DC: Department of the Navy.

US Navy. *NWP 27-3, Airborne Mine Countermeasures*. Washington, DC: Department of the Navy.

Initial Distribution List

Combined Arms Research Library
U.S. Army Command and General Staff College
Fort Leavenworth, Kansas, 66027-6900

Defense Technical Information Center
Cameron Station
Alexandria, Virginia, 22314

Marine Corps Staff College
Breckenridge Library
Marine Corps Combat Development Center
Quantico, Virginia, 22134

Naval War College Library
Hewitt Hall
U.S. Naval War College
Newport, Rhode Island, 02841-5010

Lieutenant Colonel Richard I. Kendall
Center for Army Tactics
U.S. Army Command and General Staff College
Fort Leavenworth, Kansas, 66027-6900

Major William P. Huben
Department of Joint and Combined Operations
U.S. Army Command and General Staff College
Fort Leavenworth, Kansas, 66027-6900

Lieutenant Colonel Ernest M. Pitt
200 Home Federal Building
1500 Carter Avenue
Ashland, Kentucky, 41101

www.ingramcontent.com/pod-product-compliance
Lightning Source LLC
Chambersburg PA
CBHW080248170426
43192CB00014BA/2599